JILL NORMAN
THE
CLASSIC
HERB
COOKBOOK

JILL NORMAN
THE
CLASSIC
HERB
COOKBOOK

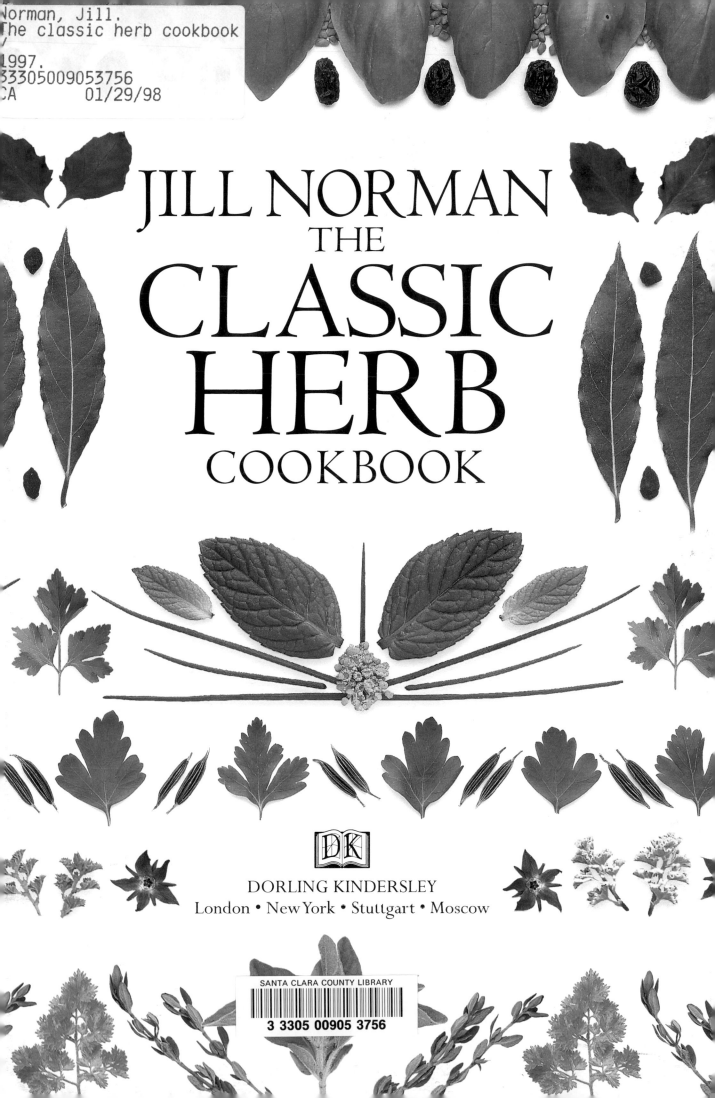

DORLING KINDERSLEY
London • New York • Stuttgart • Moscow

A DK PUBLISHING BOOK

Project Editor
Pamela Brown

Art Editor
Julia Worth

Editorial Assistant
Lorraine Turner

US Editors
Laaren Brown, Joan Whitman

Managing Editor
Fay Franklin

Managing Art Editor
Virginia Walter

Deputy Art Director
Carole Ash

Photography
Ian O'Leary

Home Economists
Nicola Fowler, Oona van den Berg, Sunil Vijayakar

Production Controller
Manjit Sihra

For Sasha and Mark

All nutritional-information figures are approximate and are based on figures from food composition tables with additional data for manufactured products, where appropriate, not on direct analysis of prepared dishes. Nutritional information is given per serving based on the number of servings in parentheses. Use these figures as a guide only. Please note that KCal is an abbreviation for kilocalories, sometimes inaccurately called calories.

First American edition, 1997
2 4 6 8 10 9 7 5 3 1

Published in the United States by DK Publishing, Inc.
95 Madison Avenue, New York, New York 10016
Visit us on the World Wide Web at http://www.dk.com

Library of Congress Cataloging-in-Publication Data

Norman, Jill
   Classic herb cookbook / by Jill Norman. -- 1st American ed.
      p.   cm.
Includes index.
ISBN 0-7894-1446-5
1. Cookery (Herbs) 2. Herbs. I. Title.
TX819.H4N6723 1996   96-35588
641.6'57--dc20   CIP

Reproduced in Italy by Scanner Services SRL
Printed and bound in Italy by A. Mondadori, Verona

CONTENTS
INTRODUCTION 6

A CATALOG OF HERBS 8

A photographic guide detailing each herb's traditional and current role, and how best to prepare and use it.

CLASSIC DISHES 48

A selection of recipes illustrating the importance of herbs in the great cuisines around the world.

RECIPES 70

A well-seasoned assortment featuring the huge range of herbs, from sweet to savory, familiar to exotic

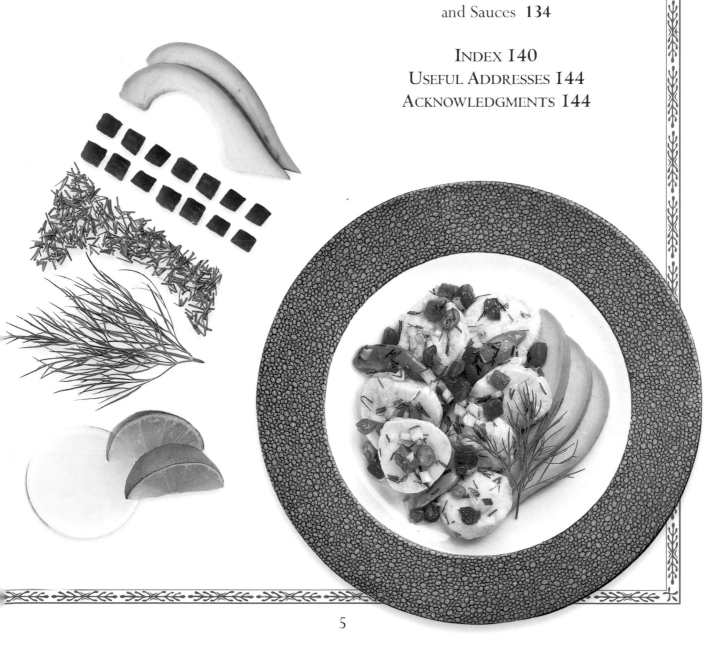

INTRODUCTION

*"Les fines herbes sont le parfum de la cuisine, mais il faut en
user avec la même discrétion que les parfums, afin de laisser
à chaque mets son goût particulier ou son individualité."*
CELESTINE EUSTIS, LA CUISINE CREOLE, *1903*

*"Herbs are the scents of the kitchen, and must be used as subtly as other scents
so that each dish retains its particular flavor and character."*

The herb gardens of the past were orderly collections of plants
for the kitchen and stillroom, for medicines, cosmetics, and
for strewing among bedlinen. Pot, salad, and aromatic herbs were
cultivated in profusion, and more plants were picked from the wild.

The distinction between herbs and leaf vegetables was seldom made.
Herb soups, boiled puddings, and pies contained spinach, leeks, beet
tops, lettuce, and chard as well as what we call herbs. At the end of
the 17th century John Evelyn's *Acetaria* listed some 70 plants for use
in salads – "a particular combination of certain crude and fresh
Herbs" that could be dressed with oil, salt, and vinegar.

Over time, some flavors that naturally complement one another
have become "classics" in different cultures: sage with veal in Italy,
tarragon with chicken in France, mint with lamb in England, cilantro
and chilies in Mexico, basil with tomatoes everywhere. Sometimes
such traditional uses can appear arbitrary and inhibit experimentation,
but, with the cross-fertilization of cuisines, adventurous variations
occur more readily – witness the many "pesto" varieties based on
cilantro, dill, arugula, and so on.

This book is an exploration of the way herbs are used in different
cuisines. It offers suggestions for bringing new varieties or new uses
for familiar herbs into the Western repertoire. In writing it I made
some discoveries, most of them rewarding, added greatly to my herb
garden, and broadened my ideas about combinations of flavors. There
remains ample scope for further exploration.

For most dishes fresh herbs are best; they add to the appearance of a dish as well as improving its flavor. Supermarkets now carry a wide if costly range. Middle Eastern or Asian stores often have big bunches for the same price as a few supermarket sprigs. These are good places to look for new and unusual herbs, as are specialized nurseries. Most herbs are easy to grow in the garden or in pots, and have the added benefit of their fragrance and availability over a long period.

Many herbs freeze successfully for a few months: they may look wilted but will retain their flavor. In some grocery stores you will find small packs of frozen leaves that are worth searching for, as are the strong-flavored herbs like oregano and tarragon preserved in oil. The herbs that dry well are those that retain their essential oil, and if they have been grown in a warm climate their aroma and flavor will be incomparably stronger.

Some herbs develop their flavors with long cooking – bay, oregano, rosemary, sage, tarragon, thyme; others are best added at the end of cooking – basil, chervil, chives, cilantro, lemon balm, and parsley.

There are classic herb mixtures but, essentially, combining herbs and other flavorings and the amounts to use are matters of personal taste. This is not an exact science: a teaspoon of chopped herbs will do little except garnish a dish of beans, although heavy-handedness is another extreme to avoid. Be judicious, always balancing the strong flavors with the mild, and use the combinations suggested here as a basis for trying out your own ideas.

A CATALOG OF HERBS

The following pages illustrate the wide range of herbs available to the cook, starting with the most popular. Where possible, different varieties are shown with notes on their properties and possible uses. On later pages, related plants — or those with similar flavors and aromas — are grouped together. Botanical names are given throughout to aid recognition.

BASIL

Ocimum basilicum

NATIVE TO INDIA, where it is sacred to Vishnu, basil reached the Mediterranean in ancient times. Today, the air in many a Greek village is filled with a spicy aroma from pots of bush basil, although it is little used in the cooking. A tender plant, basil was raised from seed in northerly herb gardens for some 200 years, but its popularity had declined by the beginning of this century. Its recent revival is largely due to the increased interest in Provençal, Italian and, lately, Thai cooking.

ANISE BASIL
O.b. 'Anise'
Has a clear anise flavor with a hint of bitterness. Used in Southeast Asian cooking.

THAI BASIL
O.b. 'Horapha'
Clean peppery smell with hints of anise. Similar to anise basil but has narrower leaves.

PESTO SAUCE
The leaves of sweet basil are pounded with pine nuts to form the base of classic pesto sauce.

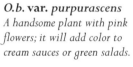

PURPLE or OPAL BASIL
O.b. var. purpurascens
A handsome plant with pink flowers; it will add color to cream sauces or green salads.

LEMON BASIL
O.b. var. citriodorum
Light green leaves have a clean lemon fragrance; good with fish and in mixed salads.

CINNAMON BASIL
O.b. 'Cinnamon'
Pink flowers and a sweet, intense scent. Stir into dried bean dishes.

LETTUCE LEAF BASIL
O.b. var. crispum
The floppy leaves can be used to wrap foods for cooking. Similar flavor to sweet basil.

PURPLE RUFFLES BASIL
O.b. 'Purple Ruffles'
The frilled leaves grow quite large and are good in salads. Use them like sweet basil. There is also a green version.

CAMPHOR BASIL
O. kilimandscharicum
Strong camphor aroma; best in herb mixtures. If hard to find, add star anise to sweet basil.

AFRICAN BLUE BASIL
O. 'African Blue'
Handsome plant with mottled purple-green leaves smelling of pepper and licorice. Use with rice, vegetables, and stews.

GREEK BASIL
O.b. var. minimum
Neat bush with small leaves and a pungent peppery aroma. Good with rice and grains.

HOLY BASIL (TULSI)
O. sanctum
Used in Thai cooking. Has notes of clove and mint and a slight bitterness. If unavailable, add a little mint to sweet basil.

SWEET BASIL
O. basilicum
The most common and popular basil; the bright green aromatic leaves can be used for all Western cooking.

AROMA & TASTE
Basil has an unmistakable spicy aroma followed by a warm flavor of clove and pepper, with notes of mint and licorice.

CULINARY USES
Best known as the base of pesto sauce of Genoa and the related pistou of southern France, basil combines well with garlic, olive oil, lemon, and tomatoes, both raw and cooked. Pepper and eggplant dishes benefit from basil, as do potatoes, beans, and rice.

To retain aroma and flavor, it is best to use only a little during cooking and to add the rest at the end. Tearing rather than chopping the leaves also helps bring out the flavor.

Sprigs of the edible flowers make an aromatic garnish or addition to a salad.

Thai cooks use three types of basil: *bai horabha* (Thai basil), the most similar to sweet basil, used in curry pastes and added to curries made with coconut milk; *bai gaprow* (holy basil), for curries without coconut milk, stir-fries, fish, and chicken dishes; and *bai manglug* (sweet balsam basil, *O. canum*), added at the end of cooking for a lemon flavor.

Basil bruises easily, so handle it carefully. It is best used fresh but can be frozen; dried or freeze-dried has little flavor. You can also preserve leaves, with a little salt between layers, in a jar of oil in the refrigerator: they will turn black, but the flavor remains for some months. A purée, made with olive oil, can be kept in the refrigerator or frozen.

For key recipes, see pages 50, 60, 90, 94, 102, 108, 138.

MINT
Mentha species

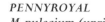

PERENNIAL PLANTS, mostly native to central Asia and the Mediterranean basin, mints hybridize easily, so there are many subspecies – and some confusion in their naming. A versatile flavoring, mint used sparingly provides a good backdrop for other herbs such as basil, dill, and parsley. In Asian cooking it blends well with spices, notably ginger, cumin, cardamom, and cloves.

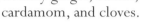

PENNYROYAL
M. pulegium (upright form)
This has an intense, almost disagreeable flavor. Formerly esteemed for stuffings and savory desserts, it must be used with caution.

PINEAPPLE MINT
M. suaveolens 'Variegata'
Its pleasant fruity flavor is suited to summer punches, fruit salads, and to flavoring ricotta or cream cheese.

APPLE MINT
M. suaveolens
Has a light flavor of apple.

BLACK PEPPERMINT
M. × piperita var. piperita
A strong, fiery flavor. Its essential oil, which contains menthol, is used for liqueurs, candies, and toothpaste.

LEMON MINT
M. piperita citrata 'Lemon'
A refreshing lemon note when you smell it. Use in salads, to make mint butter (good with grilled fish), and for drinks.

GINGER MINT
M. × gracilis 'Variegata'
Pungent and spicy: try it with black olives, feta cheese, and good bread.

EAU DE COLOGNE MINT
M. × piperita citrata
The delicate flavor goes well with vanilla to make little pots de crème. Also called lemon, orange, and bergamot mint.

BOWLES' MINT
M. × villosa alopecuroides
Wilts rapidly, but is well worth growing for its fine flavor.

MOROCCAN SPEARMINT
M. spicata 'Moroccan'
Prized for its fine aroma and taste, it is used in Morocco to flavor sweet green tea.

CURLED SPEARMINT
M. spicata 'Crispa'
Spearmint's many forms differ in color and flavor intensity. Its light fragrance is perfect for chilled pea and mint soup.

TASHKENT SPEARMINT
M. spicata 'Tashkent'
Has a concentrated aroma and flavor. An excellent choice for making fresh chutney with chilies and green mango.

AROMA & TASTE
All the mints are highly aromatic; the strong, sweetish yet fresh smell is instantly recognizable. The taste is pleasantly warm and pungent with a cooling aftertaste.

CULINARY USES
In Western cooking, mint is generally used fresh. It enhances carrots, potatoes, eggplants, and all the legumes. Its sharp yet sweet character complements grilled fish and roast or grilled lamb, whether in a marinade, as mint butter, mint sauce, or in a salsa. Add it to tomato soup with some chilies for a Latin American flavor.

Some Middle Eastern soups, stews, and stuffings call for the local pungent dried mint. A tablespoon, quickly fried in oil and added just before serving, imparts a fine fragrance to certain Turkish dishes. Sprigs of mint are always included in the bowls of herbs and salad served with *mezze* (hors d'oeuvres).

Indians combine mint with spices for vegetable and meat dishes and emphasize its cooling properties in a *raita* of yogurt and mint. This theme recurs in a cold cucumber, mint, and yogurt soup of Iran. In Vietnam, platters of mint, basil, dill, and rao ram accompany meatballs or spring rolls.

At the end of a meal, mint's clean taste goes well with fruit and in chocolate desserts. It has a natural affinity for fruit cups and punches and, of course, an American South specialty – the mint julep.

Use fresh or dried according to the dish. Mint freezes well, too.

For key recipes, see pages 56, 78, 109, 115, 124, 129.

THYME
Thymus species

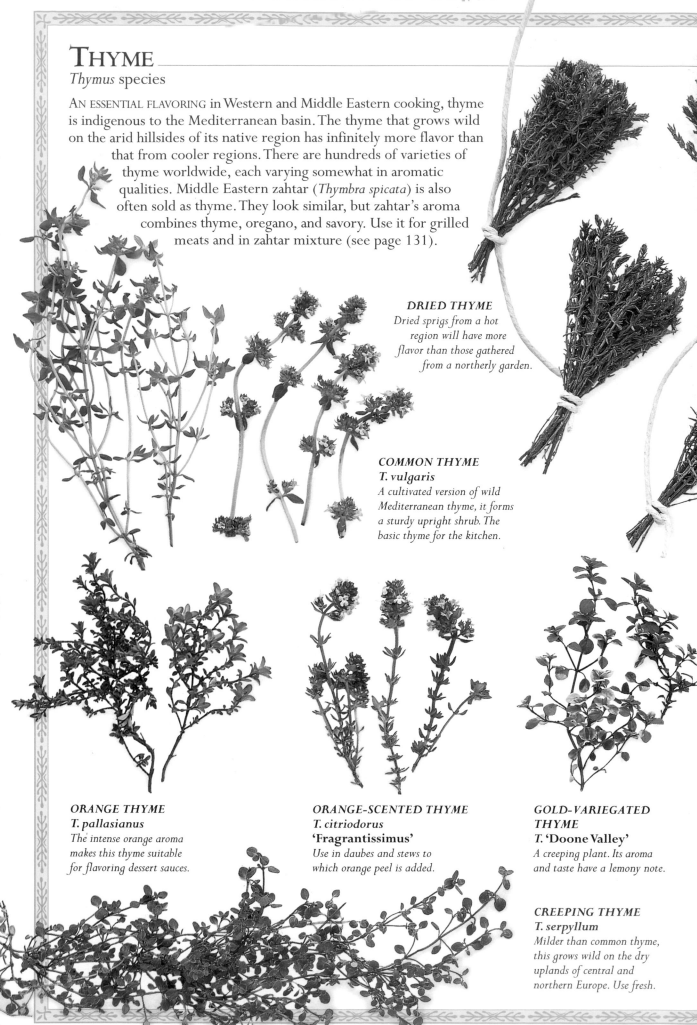

AN ESSENTIAL FLAVORING in Western and Middle Eastern cooking, thyme is indigenous to the Mediterranean basin. The thyme that grows wild on the arid hillsides of its native region has infinitely more flavor than that from cooler regions. There are hundreds of varieties of thyme worldwide, each varying somewhat in aromatic qualities. Middle Eastern zahtar (*Thymbra spicata*) is also often sold as thyme. They look similar, but zahtar's aroma combines thyme, oregano, and savory. Use it for grilled meats and in zahtar mixture (see page 131).

DRIED THYME
Dried sprigs from a hot region will have more flavor than those gathered from a northerly garden.

COMMON THYME
T. vulgaris
A cultivated version of wild Mediterranean thyme, it forms a sturdy upright shrub. The basic thyme for the kitchen.

ORANGE THYME
T. pallasianus
The intense orange aroma makes this thyme suitable for flavoring dessert sauces.

ORANGE-SCENTED THYME
T. citriodorus
'Fragrantissimus'
Use in daubes and stews to which orange peel is added.

GOLD-VARIEGATED THYME
T. 'Doone Valley'
A creeping plant. Its aroma and taste have a lemony note.

CREEPING THYME
T. serpyllum
Milder than common thyme, this grows wild on the dry uplands of central and northern Europe. Use fresh.

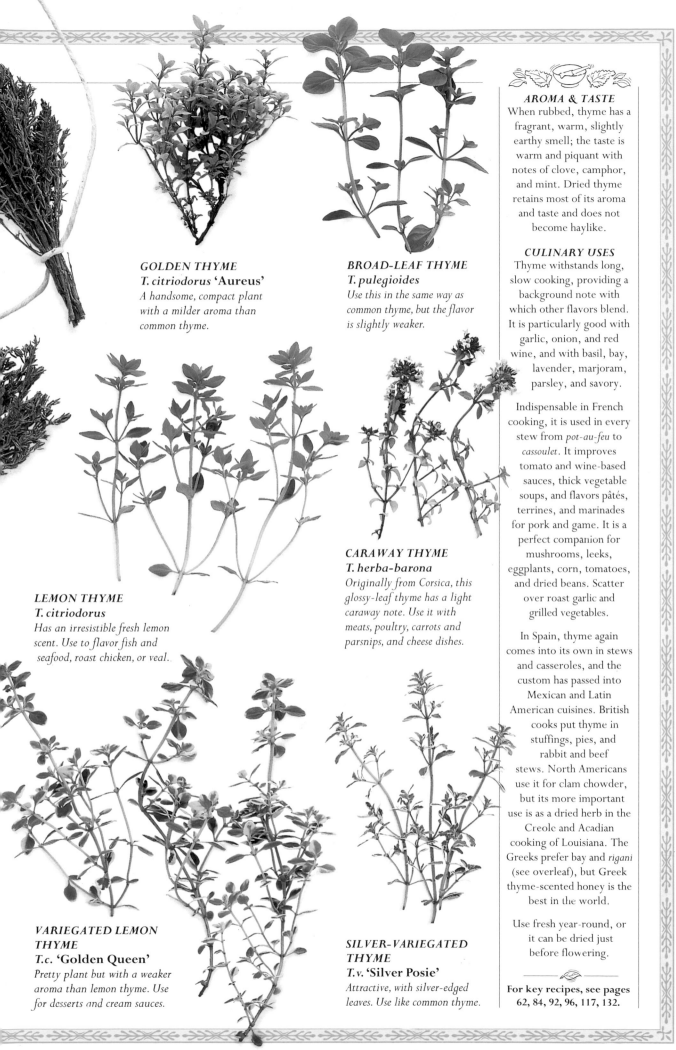

GOLDEN THYME
T. citriodorus **'Aureus'**
A handsome, compact plant with a milder aroma than common thyme.

BROAD-LEAF THYME
T. pulegioides
Use this in the same way as common thyme, but the flavor is slightly weaker.

LEMON THYME
T. citriodorus
Has an irresistible fresh lemon scent. Use to flavor fish and seafood, roast chicken, or veal.

CARAWAY THYME
T. herba-barona
Originally from Corsica, this glossy-leaf thyme has a light caraway note. Use it with meats, poultry, carrots and parsnips, and cheese dishes.

VARIEGATED LEMON THYME
T.c. **'Golden Queen'**
Pretty plant but with a weaker aroma than lemon thyme. Use for desserts and cream sauces.

SILVER-VARIEGATED THYME
T.v. **'Silver Posie'**
Attractive, with silver-edged leaves. Use like common thyme.

AROMA & TASTE
When rubbed, thyme has a fragrant, warm, slightly earthy smell; the taste is warm and piquant with notes of clove, camphor, and mint. Dried thyme retains most of its aroma and taste and does not become haylike.

CULINARY USES
Thyme withstands long, slow cooking, providing a background note with which other flavors blend. It is particularly good with garlic, onion, and red wine, and with basil, bay, lavender, marjoram, parsley, and savory.

Indispensable in French cooking, it is used in every stew from *pot-au-feu* to *cassoulet*. It improves tomato and wine-based sauces, thick vegetable soups, and flavors pâtés, terrines, and marinades for pork and game. It is a perfect companion for mushrooms, leeks, eggplants, corn, tomatoes, and dried beans. Scatter over roast garlic and grilled vegetables.

In Spain, thyme again comes into its own in stews and casseroles, and the custom has passed into Mexican and Latin American cuisines. British cooks put thyme in stuffings, pies, and rabbit and beef stews. North Americans use it for clam chowder, but its more important use is as a dried herb in the Creole and Acadian cooking of Louisiana. The Greeks prefer bay and *rigani* (see overleaf), but Greek thyme-scented honey is the best in the world.

Use fresh year-round, or it can be dried just before flowering.

For key recipes, see pages 62, 84, 92, 96, 117, 132.

MARJORAM AND OREGANO
Origanum species

THESE CLOSELY RELATED plants have entirely different characteristics for the cook. Sweet marjoram is a fragrant plant that will enhance almost any food. Wild marjoram, *O. vulgare*, a highly variable species, grows from the Himalayas to the British Isles, and in North America. The peppery Mediterranean varieties are commonly called oregano. In Mexico and the Caribbean a number of unrelated plants are also called oregano.

MEXICAN OREGANO
Lippia graveolens
One of the plants commonly known as Mexican oregano (see page 43). Very aromatic, it goes well with hot peppers.

GOLDEN MARJORAM
O. vulgare 'Aurea'
A striking plant with dense foliage and white or mauve flowers and a mild aroma.

SMALL-LEAVED OREGANO
O. microphyllum
A native of Crete with the same characteristics as O. vulgare.

WILD MARJORAM
O. vulgare
Innocuous and grassy when grown in cool climates. For flavor, choose a southern subspecies such as hirtum.

GREEK OREGANO
O. vulgare sp.
The most intensely aromatic. Many varieties, cultivated and wild, are sold dried and ground under the Greek name rigani.

SWEET MARJORAM
O. majorana
*Also called knotted marjoram,
from the look of the buds, this
is a pretty plant. It tastes
sweeter than pot marjoram.*

POT MARJORAM
O. onites
*This has a piquant, bitter
note. It is sometimes referred
to as Sicilian oregano.*

**CURLED GOLDEN
MARJORAM**
O.v. 'Aureum Crispum'
*Forms a compact plant
with crinkled, mild-
flavored leaves.*

CRETAN DITTANY
O. dictamnus
*The thick silvery leaves — fresh
or dried — are mainly used for
a tea, but they also flavor
meat and vegetable dishes.*

CUBAN OREGANO
Plectranthus sp.
*Used as oregano in the
Caribbean and Mexico, this
fleshy succulent has a clean
oregano aroma (see page 43).*

AROMA & TASTE
Marjoram has a sweet, subtle spiciness; the taste is warm, lightly spicy, bitterish with a note of camphor. Oregano is more robust, with an intense pepperiness and a distinct bite.

CULINARY USES
Marjoram is a highly desirable herb, used in a wide variety of dishes. Its delicate flavor is easily lost in cooking, so add it only at the last moment. Put leaves and flower knots into salads, serve with mozzarella and other young cheeses, and with anchovies, as they do in Italy. It is an ideal flavoring for artichokes, broccoli, zucchini, mushrooms, onions, for eggs and all poultry. With parsley and lemon thyme it makes an excellent stuffing for poultry or fish.

Oregano's penetrating aroma is most obviously associated with Italian cooking, especially tomato sauce, pizza, and *pizzaiola* sauce. But its use along the Mediterranean is widespread, and the dried herb is often preferred. In Greece it is used for *souvlaki*, baked fish, and Greek salad. In Spain it appears in stews of lamb, chicken, or vegetables. Use it for hearty stews, beans, ratatouille, pasta sauces, for marinades and bouquets garnis, and for flavored oils and vinegars. The aroma develops with long cooking.

Marjoram dried in bud retains its strength for some months; it also freezes well. Dried oregano retains its strength for a year or more; buy Greek, Italian, or Spanish.

For recipes, see pages 113, 114, 116, 120 for marjoram; 62, 92, 100 for oregano.

PARSLEY
Petroselinum crispum

NATIVE TO THE eastern Mediterranean, this biennial herb is used extensively in Western and Middle Eastern cooking. There are curly and flat-leaf varieties, the former most common in northerly climates, the latter throughout southern Europe and the Middle East. Curly parsley is attractive as a garnish, but flat-leaf parsley has the edge when it comes to flavor. Hamburg parsley is grown in central and eastern Europe, where it is prized for its edible roots.

ITALIAN PARSLEY
P.c. 'Italian'
Flat-leaf varieties have fine flavor and are generally preferred for cooking.

FLAT-LEAF PARSLEY
Parsley helps highlight other flavors and is an excellent foil for garlic. It is rich in vitamins A and C, in iron, and in calcium.

CURLY PARSLEY
Use for garnishes or to achieve an attractive green color in a mayonnaise or sauce without a dominant parsley flavor.

MITSUBA (JAPANESE PARSLEY)
Cryptotaenia japonica
This cool climate perennial is an important flavoring in Japan (see page 41).

HAMBURG PARSLEY
P.c. var. tuberosum
Can be grated raw into salads, used to flavor soups and stews, or cooked as a root vegetable — it makes a fine purée.

AROMA & TASTE
Parsley has a fresh, slightly spicy aroma and a tangy flavor with a light peppery note. The aroma of flat-leaf parsley is finer than that of curly and the flavor stronger and more persistent. Stems have a more intense flavor than leaves; for long cooking, use a bundle of stems, then remove them and add chopped leaves before serving. The flavor of Hamburg parsley root is somewhere between celeriac and parsley. (Parsnips are not related.)

CULINARY USES
In Anglo-Saxon cultures parsley has only recently moved beyond being used purely as decoration — "planted like trees in a garden of cold meat," wrote Tom Stobart in *Herbs, Spices, and Flavorings* — to being a flavoring.

In French cuisine it is essential in a bouquet garni or mixture of *fines herbes*. Finely chopped leaves are added to savory butters, a *persillade* (see page 135) or its Catalan equivalent, a *picada* (see page 135). Italians put parsley into stuffings with lemon, bread crumbs, garlic, and capers, and into *salsa verde* (see page 139).

In Turkey a parsley omelet heralds spring; in Morocco parsley is served in a salad with onion and lemon; and throughout the Middle East tabbouleh, a salad of cracked wheat and parsley, is a mainstay. Deep-fried sprigs of parsley are a delicious garnish for fish, or try it dipped in tempura batter.

Use parsley fresh; it can be frozen for winter use.

For key recipes, see pages 56, 74, 90, 97, 108, 114, 138.

CILANTRO
Coriandrum sativum

PROBABLY THE MOST widely used herb in the world, cilantro has been prized for its flavoring and medicinal properties for thousands of years. It is both herb and spice, for the orange-scented seeds, called coriander, have their own value in savory and sweet dishes. In China it is known as the "fragrant plant"; there and throughout Southeast Asia the leaves and roots are most in demand. In India and the Middle East, both leaf and seed are used; and it is the key flavoring, with chilies, in Mexican and Latin American cooking.

RAO RAM (VIETNAMESE CILANTRO)
Polygonum odoratum
An herb used in Far Eastern cooking (see page 41).

LEAVES
These are fanlike and more rounded than flat-leaf parsley, although the two are sometimes confused. The smell soon indicates the difference.

SEEDS
Ripe seeds are used in curries, vegetables à la grecque, pickles, desserts, and cakes; unripe are used in sauces and marinades.

ROOTS
More earthy and musky than leaves, roots add depth of flavor. Traditional in Thai curries, try them also in stews and with braised meat or fish.

AROMA & TASTE
Leaves and unripe fruits have a distinctive fetid smell, which is quite addictive; the flavor is earthy with a suggestion of parsley and mint and a lemony note. The ripe seeds are very different, with a sweet cedar-and-sandalwood aroma and a mild orange-peel taste. The roots smell musky and faintly of citrus.

CULINARY USES
Cilantro teams with virtually any savory food; it has an affinity for garlic, basil, mint, parsley, lemon and lime, chilies, and coconut.

India and Mexico both use the excellent combination of cilantro and green chilies in chutneys, relishes, and salsas. In China it appears with ginger and scallions in stir-fried dishes; in Vietnam it is always on the herb and salad plate with basil, dill, mint, and rao ram. The roots go into Thai curry paste; the leaves are used with basil, chilies, and coconut milk.

In the Middle East its companions are nuts and spices; the seeds and leaves may both be used in the same dish. The Portuguese use cilantro with potatoes, fava beans, and their excellent clams.

Cilantro is superb with fish and seafood, with beans, chickpeas, plantains, rice, root vegetables, and squash. It is best added toward the end of cooking to preserve flavor.

Use leaves fresh; roots can be washed, wrapped in paper, and refrigerated. Both freeze well.

For key recipes, see pages 60, 68, 87, 90, 120, 138.

SAGE
Salvia species

A SMALL PERENNIAL bush, sage grows best on the poor dry soils of southern Europe, its native habitat. It is hardy enough to survive in most areas north of the Alps and is widely cultivated in North America. Aromatic strength varies according to soil and climate.

PURPLE SAGE
S.o. 'Purpurea'
Intensely aromatic but less hardy than common sage.

GREEK SAGE
S. fruticosa
More spicy than common sage. Used in Greece to make tea.

CLARY SAGE
S. sclarea
The huge, wrinkled leaves make tasty fritters served with sugar.

CLARY SAGE FLOWERS
The flowers of this strongly aromatic biennial make it a handsome plant.

COMMON SAGE
S. officinalis
There are broad and narrow-leaf varieties, the latter with stunning purplish blue flowers.

DRIED SAGE
Has a medicinal, musty smell and is best used for tea.

PINEAPPLE SAGE
S. elegans
Has a pineapple scent; use with fish, in salads, and fruit drinks.

AROMA & TASTE
Sage smells and tastes of camphor, with a note of bitterness and a warm, sometimes burning, spiciness. Its flavor is crude and overpowering to some people.

CULINARY USES
Use fresh sage but use it cautiously. It is best with meats, especially fat meats such as pork, lamb, duck, and goose, and strongly flavored fish.

Its use in Italy is widespread: with liver and veal, in *focaccia*, to make fritters, to flavor polenta. With butter and Parmesan, a few leaves make an excellent pasta sauce. Fried leaves make a good vegetable garnish. In southern France it makes a warming sage and garlic soup; in northern Europe sage accompanies eel and pike; in Britain it is best known in stuffing and in sage Derby cheese.

Sage can be dried but is best used fresh.

For key recipes, see pages 96, 100, 120, 128, 129, 133.

MYRTLE
Myrtus communis

A FRAGRANT EVERGREEN, native to the mountain regions of the Mediterranean basin, myrtle has white flowers and aromatic dark purple berries. In cool climates it needs protection in winter.

MYRTLE SPRIGS
An ornamental bush that deserves to be grown more widely. Put some sprigs on the embers while grilling to perfume food. The compact M.c. subsp. tarentina (near right) is native to Corsica and Sardinia.

AROMA & TASTE
The slightly resinous aroma has similarities with juniper and allspice; the taste is like juniper and faintly astringent.

CULINARY USES
Used in much the same way as bay. Combine with thyme to flavor meat and game, and with fennel for fish. Discard the leaves on serving. Use for marinades and in pickles. In southern Italy fresh cheeses are wrapped in myrtle leaves to add flavor.

ROSEMARY
Rosmarinus officinalis

THE MOST BEAUTIFUL and aromatic of all herbs, rosemary is a dense evergreen shrub with needlelike leaves and pale blue flowers. It gives off an intense fragrance when touched. Native to the Mediterranean, rosemary thrives in the thin upland soils of southern Europe and grows best by the sea.

WHITE ROSEMARY
Use the attractive white, pink, or, more usual, blue flowers as garnishes and in salads.

PINK ROSEMARY
Put rosemary on the barbecue embers when grilling, or use a branch to baste the food on the grill.

BLUE ROSEMARY
The gray-green leaves offset the flowers admirably. Use sprigs that can be removed at the end of cooking to avoid chewing on the spiky leaves.

AROMA & TASTE
The aroma of rosemary is assertive, with notes of camphor and pine, a hint of nutmeg and lavender. Camphor and nutmeg are present in the taste.

CULINARY USES
The favorite herb in Italy, where it is sometimes used to excess. Rosemary combines well with thyme and bay, with garlic and wine. Put a sprig under a roast of pork or lamb, and in marinades for rabbit and game. It goes well with oily fish such as sardines or mackerel, with eggplants, beans, cabbage, zucchini, potatoes, and tomatoes.

Rosemary can be dried and crumbled but is better used fresh.

For key recipes, see pages 96, 100, 120, 125, 132.

BAY
Laurus nobilis

NATIVE TO THE eastern Mediterranean, bay trees have long been cultivated in northern Europe. They need a sheltered spot but, should they die back in a very cold winter, the roots will often put out new shoots the following spring.

DRIED LEAVES
Most commonly used in cooking, the aroma is less strong than that of fresh. Keep whole or break into large pieces to remove on serving, or crumble.

FRESH LEAVES
These are more likely to be used in marinades and pickles. When first picked, they taste slightly bitter, but this fades within a few days.

AROMA & TASTE
Bay has a fresh, sweet balsamic aroma with a spicy note.

CULINARY USES
Basic to much European cooking, bay leaves go into marinades, pickled herrings, Italian vegetables preserved in oil or vinegar, bouquets garnis, and *court bouillons*. They are infused in milk to make béchamel, give a deep flavor to tomato sauce, and perform well with braised meats and in all slow-cooked dishes. Put a leaf and some lemon zest into pears poached in red wine; use bay to give a delicate flavor to creams and custards.

Dry bay leaves in the dark to retain their color.

For key recipes, see pages 82, 96, 97, 101, 105, 135.

GARLIC AND CHIVES
Allium species

THOUGHT TO BE of central Asian origin, the onion family encompasses some 500 members. Most are edible, but not all are good to eat. Many still grow wild; others have been cultivated for thousands of years. The flavors of the onion tribe are perhaps those most taken for granted in the kitchen. After onions, garlic is the most widely used. The Koreans hold the record for consumption per capita, followed by the Southeast Asians, then the peoples around the Mediterranean. This is the home of *aïoli*, *skordalia*, *tarator*, and other garlic-based sauces and dressings.

FRESH GARLIC
A. sativum
Young or "wet" garlic is juicy with a gentle flavor. It is excellent braised or roasted whole, alone or with new potatoes.

CHIVES
A. schoenoprasum
The smallest and mildest member of the family. Use fresh, as chives wilt quickly and the aroma fades when cooked.

WELSH ONION
A. fistulosum
Also called oriental bunching onions, these are Asia's largest onion crop. Varieties can have either white or red stems.

ROCAMBOLE (SANDLEEK)
A. sativum var. ophioscordon
Cut the slender leaves (left) like chives, and chop the small bulb (above). Use the tiny cloves that form in the flowerhead as garlic.

DRIED GARLIC
Choose unbruised firm heads; in winter remove indigestible green shoots. Use the flat blade of a knife to crush dried cloves; a press can give an acrid taste.

PURPLE GARLIC
Garlic may have violet, pink, or white skin, depending on variety. You can snip young shoots as you would chives.

CHIVE FLOWERS
These have a pleasant, light onion fragrance and taste, and are attractive scattered over a salad or added to omelets.

CHINESE CHIVES
A. tuberosum
Grown throughout Asia; the flat leaves and white buds have a distinctive garlic flavor. Bud stems and yellow blanched leaves are considered a delicacy.

AROMA & TASTE
Chives have a light onion aroma and spicy onion flavor. Chinese chives are more garlicky. The flavor of Welsh onions lies between leeks and onions. Dried garlic is pungent, hot, sometimes acrid, but the flavor mellows in cooking. Rocambole tastes like a delicate garlic.

CULINARY USES
Scatter chives over soups and salads, add to egg dishes, mix with soft cheese or yogurt, and combine with parsley, tarragon, and chervil for *fines herbes*.

Chinese chives, cut into short lengths and quickly blanched or stir-fried, keep their color and flavor. Use in spring rolls, with tofu, bean sprouts, eggs, noodles, and in stir-fried dishes with beef or shrimp.

Both bulbs and tops of Welsh onions can be used. Essential for Asian cooking, they can be added to Western stews, potato, and bean dishes shortly before the end of cooking.

In European cooking, garlic is roasted with chicken and lamb, baked in wine, puréed, blanched, or sautéed; raw, it flavors salads, is rubbed over bread with tomato and oil, pounded with egg yolks and oil to make *aïoli*, or with nuts and basil to make pesto. In Asia, its companions are lemongrass, fresh ginger, cilantro, and chili peppers.

Wrap Chinese chives and Welsh onions to prevent their smell from spreading. Keep garlic in a cool dry place, not the refrigerator.

For key recipes, see pages 78, 79, 94, 113 for chives; 82, 96, 106, 134 for garlic.

FENNEL

Foeniculum vulgare

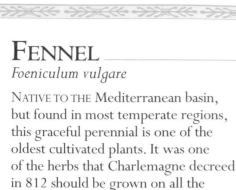

NATIVE TO THE Mediterranean basin, but found in most temperate regions, this graceful perennial is one of the oldest cultivated plants. It was one of the herbs that Charlemagne decreed in 812 should be grown on all the imperial estates. All parts are edible.

GREEN FENNEL
Use stalks and leaves to flavor court bouillon and marinades for fish. Snip leaves with scissors; do not chop.

BRONZE FENNEL
The reddish fronds blend handsomely with the green in a garden border. It has a milder aroma and flavor.

SEEDS
The seeds contain a high proportion of anethole, which accounts for the similarity of flavor with anise, but they are more astringent.

AROMA & TASTE
Fennel has a warm anise-licorice aroma and taste with a slight sweetness and a hint of camphor.

CULINARY USES
A traditional flavoring for fish; early cookbooks recommend serving fennel sauce with oily fish. In Provence, red mullet, bream, and bass are grilled or baked with fresh or dried stalks. It is essential to Sicilian *pasta con le sarde* and has an affinity for rice, lentils, potatoes, cabbage, and beets. The Italians roast pork with the seed and use it to flavor *finocchiona*, the renowned salami of Florence.

Leaves are best fresh; dried stalks keep for a season.

For recipes, see pages 84, 97, 101, 106, 118.

CHERVIL

Anthriscus cerefolium

"SWEET CHERVIL IS so like in taste unto Anis seede that it much delighteth the taste among other herbs in a sallet" (Parkinson, *Paradisus*, 1629). Much appreciated in France, Germany, and Holland, its arrival in the markets signals springtime, and chervil soup and sauces appear on menus. Elsewhere it deserves to be better known.

LEAVES
Chervil is easy to grow in the garden from seed. Pick outer leaves first; the inner ones will keep on growing. The lacy foliage fades to pale cream and pink as it dies off.

AROMA & TASTE
The smell is sweet, the taste soothing; both are a subtle blend of anise, tarragon, and caraway. Chervil brings out the flavors of other herbs, most clearly in the classic *fines herbes* blend with parsley, tarragon, and chives.

CULINARY USES
Chervil has an affinity for eggs, fish, poultry, veal, green beans, carrots mushrooms, and potatoes. Use lavishly and add it toward the end of cooking, since the flavor dissipates quickly. Chervil gives a delicate taste to vinaigrettes and sauces.

Use fresh, although it can be frozen for a few weeks. All flavor fades if dried.

For recipes, see pages 74, 78, 79, 90, 106, 116.

ANISE
Pimpinella anisum

ANISE HAS BEEN cultivated for centuries. Our ancestors grew it for its digestive properties; in medieval times, anise comfits (sugar-coated seeds) were taken after rich meals; in India today the seeds are chewed to aid digestion and freshen the breath. Anethole oil from the seeds is used in anise-flavored aperitifs and liqueurs.

AROMA & TASTE
Anise, the strongest of the anise-type herbs, has a refined licorice-like aroma and taste with sweet, mildly peppery undertones.

CULINARY USES
Use young anise leaves in salads, and chopped leaves and young stems to flavor carrots, parsnips, pumpkin, and chestnuts, or to make tea. A mixture of leaves and seeds makes a fresh flavoring for rich meats such as pork and duck. Anise-flavored aperitifs and liqueurs are well worth keeping in the kitchen to enliven fish, shellfish, and vegetable dishes.

Use fresh leaves only; seeds are used dried.

For recipes, see pages 79, 115.

LEAVES
Anise has fine, feathery leaves with clusters of white flowers in late summer. It can be grown from seed quite easily and plants are sometimes available from nurseries.

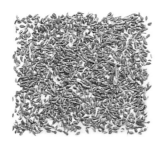

SEEDS
The seeds give a spicy note to breads and desserts, and can be used in marinades for seafood and in sauces. Commercially, they are used in candies.

DILL
Anethum graveolens

DILL HAS BEEN grown for its leaves and seeds since antiquity. In the Middle Ages it was held to be a magic herb that would guard against witchcraft. Indigenous to central Asia and southern Europe, its main producers today are Scandinavia, Poland, Russia, Turkey, and Italy.

LEAVES
Dill loses its fine aroma in cooking, so is best added at the last moment. Snip rather than chop the leaves.

AROMA & TASTE
Dill leaves have a fragrant aniselike aroma with a lemony note; the flavor is of anise, mild but sustained. The seeds smell almost like caraway; the taste is warm and slightly sharp.

CULINARY USES
The fresh, clean taste marries well with fish and seafood, especially salmon. It enhances scrambled or baked eggs and makes a fine salad with cucumber and sour cream. In Greece, dill is added to spinach; in Turkey and the Middle East it flavors zucchini, potatoes, fava beans, and rice.

Best fresh, but freezes well. Dried has little aroma or flavor.

For recipes, see pages 52, 54, 76, 104, 109, 120.

SEEDS
The seeds are used in cakes and breads, soups and stews, and for pickling. Pickled cucumbers, or dill pickles, are favorites in many countries.

ANGELICA

Angelica archangelica

PROBABLY NATIVE to the Middle East, but for centuries grown even in far northern Europe, angelica is a vigorous, handsome biennial that grows up to 7ft (2m) tall. It makes a showy plant with its bright green serrated leaves and huge domes of tiny pale yellow-green flowers. All parts are aromatic and edible.

DRIED LEAVES
The leaves may be dried and used in baking and for making an herbal tea, but little remains of the aroma or flavor of fresh angelica leaves.

STEMS
France has long had an important industry in candying young angelica stems, but they are becoming increasingly difficult to find.

AROMA & TASTE
A crushed leaf gives off a pleasantly sweet, musky scent. The overall taste is again musky with a warm aftertaste, but the young stems and leaves can also be bittersweet and sharp.

CULINARY USES
Young, juicy stems can be eaten fresh or boiled as a vegetable. Chopped young leaves can be added sparingly to salads, to a young white cheese, or used to stuff fish. Leaves stewed with rhubarb reduce its acidity. Oil distilled from the seeds and roots is used to flavor vermouths and liqueurs of the Benedictine type.

Use fresh angelica; dried leaves have a much reduced flavor.

For recipes, see pages 79, 115, 116.

CELERY

Apium graveolens

WILD CELERY, or smallage, is a common European plant from which cultivated celery was developed. By 1800, three kinds were known: garden celery, with fleshy white or green stems, round-rooted celeriac, and cutting celery, closest in appearance to wild celery.

CUTTING CELERY
Used year-round as a flavoring herb in northern Europe. It looks very much like flat-leaf parsley; only smelling it reveals the difference.

WATER CELERY
Oenanthe stolonifera
Also called water dropwort and Vietnamese celery. Young shoots are highly prized in winter in Southeast Asia and Japan.

CHINESE CELERY
Chinese celery (kun choi) looks similar to cutting celery; it is widely grown in China and used as a vegetable and as a flavoring herb.

AROMA & TASTE
The taste of cutting and Chinese celery is warm yet somewhat rank and bitter, but it mellows with cooking. Water celery is milder, reminiscent of both celery and parsley.

CULINARY USES
Seldom eaten raw, cutting celery is added to many soups and stews, often along with celeriac. In China, leaves and stalks are used in soups, vegetable dishes, and stir-fries. In Vietnam, finely chopped water celery is used raw to flavor salads, or briefly cooked and added to soups and fish or chicken dishes. In Japan it is also used for *sukiyaki*.

Use fresh celery only.

For recipes, see pages 106, 112.

CARAWAY
Carum carvi

CARAWAY HAS BEEN cultivated throughout Europe since medieval times; it is native to northern and central Europe and Asia. Today Holland, Germany, Poland, and Russia are the main producers, but it is also an important crop in Canada and the United States. All parts of the plant are edible but, commercially, caraway is grown for its seeds.

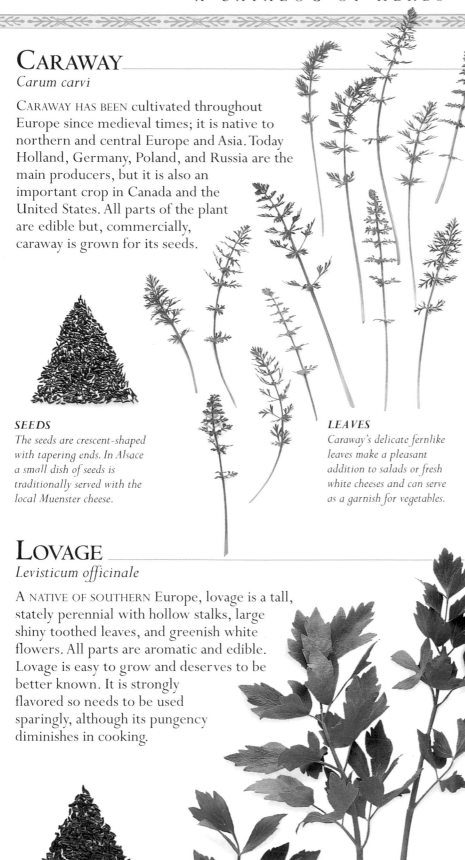

SEEDS
The seeds are crescent-shaped with tapering ends. In Alsace a small dish of seeds is traditionally served with the local Muenster cheese.

LEAVES
Caraway's delicate fernlike leaves make a pleasant addition to salads or fresh white cheeses and can serve as a garnish for vegetables.

AROMA & TASTE
The aroma combines elements of dill, anise, and cumin with a note of lemon. The taste is similar, warming and slightly bitter. The seeds have the strongest flavor.

CULINARY USES
Caraway combines well with parsley and thyme. In central European and Jewish cooking, the seeds are put into soups, cabbage, sauerkraut, and potato dishes; Hungarians add them to goulash, Germans and Austrians to meat stews. Caraway is used to flavor cheeses, sausages, breads, especially dark rye breads, and cakes. The liqueur Kümmel is flavored with caraway.

Use the leaves fresh.

For recipes, see pages 79, 115.

LOVAGE
Levisticum officinale

A NATIVE OF SOUTHERN Europe, lovage is a tall, stately perennial with hollow stalks, large shiny toothed leaves, and greenish white flowers. All parts are aromatic and edible. Lovage is easy to grow and deserves to be better known. It is strongly flavored so needs to be used sparingly, although its pungency diminishes in cooking.

SEEDS
Lovage seeds dry well. They have a sweeter flavor than the leaves and are useful for adding to breads, pickles, sauces, and marinades.

LEAVES
These are used fresh or blanched in salads and for sauces, stuffings, and stews. They can be dried, but their taste is more intensely yeasty.

AROMA & TASTE
There is some similarity to celery, but lovage is more piquant and has musky overtones with notes of anise, lemon, and yeast. Dishes flavored with lovage need less salt.

CULINARY USES
Lovage seems to give body to dishes; it is particularly good with rice, beans, and vegetables. It makes an excellent soup and its flavor goes well with smoked fish. Try lovage butter with potatoes or shred a few leaves into a tomato or egg dish. The blanched stalks can be eaten as a vegetable, dressed with vinaigrette.

Fresh leaves are best. Seeds may be dried.

For recipes, see pages 74, 115, 116, 138.

HORSERADISH

Armoracia rusticana

HORSERADISH IS EASILY recognizable by its large wrinkled leaves, which grow straight up from the root, and in summer by its white flower spike. It grows easily and is invasive if not dug up regularly. Indigenous to eastern Europe, it has long been appreciated in the cooking of Russia, central Europe, and Scandinavia. It often serves as the "bitter herb" of Passover Seders.

ROOT
This is scrubbed and grated, but fresh horseradish is not easy to find. Dried flaked root is better than most of the oversweetened preparations on sale.

LEAVES
The leaves are pungent when crushed. Although it is normally the root that is eaten, a few tender young leaves can be used to give a sharp taste to a salad.

AROMA & TASTE
Extremely pungent when grated, but this dissipates rapidly, so prepare just before eating. The taste is sharply mustardy. If cooked, the volatile oils are driven off and so no pungency develops.

CULINARY USES
Grated, it can be put into beet and potato salads. It is more usually blended with cream, vinegar, and sugar to make a sauce, and is a condiment often offered with roast beef. "Prepared" horseradish, grated and sold in jars, is a favorite with cold cuts and smoked fish. Serve, too, with oily fish.

Horseradish keeps for 2–3 weeks in the refrigerator. It can be grated and frozen.

For a recipe, see page 79.

CURRY PLANT

Helichrysum italicum

THIS DECORATIVE PERENNIAL, a native of southern Europe, will grow up to 2ft (60cm) in a sunny position. The silver-gray downy leaves and bright yellow flowers set off the green plants of the herb garden. It gives off a warm spicy smell when rubbed.

LEAVES
The curry plant's silvery needlelike leaves and shrubby habit make it a handsome edging in a formal garden.

AROMA & TASTE
When crushed, the plant has a distinct scent of curry with a hint of sweetness. The taste is less aromatic. The flowers have a similar, milder fragrance.

CULINARY USES
Never used for curry, in spite of its name, and only used straight from the plant. A sprig or two of curry plant added to thick vegetable soups, to lamb and pork stews, and to rice and to pickles, will give them an elusive and subtle spicy flavor. Remove the sprig before serving.

Curry plant leaves are best used fresh.

FENUGREEK
Trigonella foenum-graecum

NATIVE TO THE eastern Mediterranean, the plant's botanical name, *foenum-graecum*, means Greek hay. A good source of vitamins, proteins, and minerals, fenugreek is useful in a vegetarian diet. The seeds are used as a spice in the Middle East and in India, where they are a constituent of curry powder.

SEEDS
The strongly aromatic seeds can be sprouted. Use these shoots raw in small quantities in salads, or steam or stir-fry.

LEAVES
This robust annual is easy to grow in mild climates and is a good addition to the herb garden. Picked fresh, the leaves are excellent in salads.

AROMA & TASTE
Fresh fenugreek is mildly pungent and slightly bitter. Aroma and taste are intensified in the dried leaves, and there is a fragrant hint of hay.

CULINARY USES
The bitter flavor of the leaves is much valued in India, where they are cooked with potatoes, and with spinach and other greens, or chopped and added to the dough for *chapatis* or *puris*. In Iran, fenugreek leaves, fresh or dried, are used in herb stews and flavorings for meat.

Use fresh from the garden, or buy dried leaves from Indian or Iranian stores. The Indian name is *methi*, the Iranian *shamba-lileh*.

For recipes, see pages 79, 96, 108, 133.

MUSTARD
Brassica juncea

MUSTARD SEEDS ARE perhaps the most important temperate-climate spice crop, and several varieties of leaf are eaten as a vegetable in China and the southern United States. However, only in central Europe is mustard generally considered to have potential as an herb.

SEEDS
Brown mustard seeds are the kind most used for commercial mustard production. They can also be crushed and used in herb oil and vinegar dressings.

LEAVES
The mustard plant has dark green leaves, the larger ones toothed like arugula. The seed pods that follow the small yellow flowers are smooth or hairy depending on variety.

AROMA & TASTE
The leaves have distinct pungency and a warm peppery taste; the yellow flowers have a mild mustard flavor.

CULINARY USES
The young leaves make a fine addition to green salads; different varieties of mustard seedlings — purple, green, and beautiful, feathery Japanese mizuna — are grown commercially for salad mixtures. They are also easy to raise in the garden.

Shredded leaves make a pleasant garnish for beets, carrots, celeriac, zucchini, and potato and tomato salads. Add them to a ham or beef sandwich or to a dish of stir-fried vegetables.

Use fresh leaves only.

BORAGE
Borago officinalis

AN ANNUAL OF southern European origin, borage thrives on chalky soils throughout Europe and North America. In the past it was said to make people cheerful and courageous; research has now shown that it stimulates the adrenal glands.

LEAVES
Shred the coarse prickly leaves unless they are being used as an aromatic garnish.

FLOWERS
These look beautiful floating on a creamy soup or in a salad. They can also be crystallized in syrup to use for desserts.

AROMA & TASTE
Borage has a light aroma and stronger taste of cucumber; it is slightly tart, cool, and fresh.

CULINARY USES
Shred young leaves for salads (especially with cucumber), dressings, sauces, and salsas. Borage combines well with yogurt, sour cream, and fresh white cheeses. Add to soups in the last few minutes if served warm. In northern Italy it is sautéed and used with spinach and other herbs in risottos and pasta fillings. Among the herbs, team it with anise, burnet, dill, or garlic. Use in fruit, alcohol, or yogurt-based summer drinks.

Use borage sparingly and always fresh.

For recipes, see pages 73, 108, 115.

LEMON VERBENA
Aloysia triphylla

LEMON VERBENA IS a shrub native to South America. Brought to Europe in the 17th century, it was much planted in Mediterranean gardens. Its intense fragrance was soon taken up in the manufacturing of toilet waters; its culinary career came later, first as a tea, then as an alternative to lemon juice.

LEAVES
The narrow, rough-textured leaves are tough to chew, so chop them fine or remove before serving. Dried leaves are only good for tea, and fresh would be better.

AROMA & TASTE
Lemon verbena has an enticing aroma of fresh, sharp lemon. The taste is less strong, but the aroma is long lasting.

CULINARY USES
It is excellent with fish and poultry – put some sprigs into the cavity of a fish or chicken; add it to stuffing for pork. Try it in a pilaf with lemon zest and toasted pine nuts, or with carrots, mushrooms, or squash. Combine it with lemon thyme or balm. It makes a fresh-scented sorbet or ice cream, and can be chopped for fruit tarts and desserts. A few leaves flavor a jar of sugar.

Lemon verbena leaves can be frozen.

For recipes, see pages 79, 122, 125, 129, 136.

FRENCH TARRAGON

Artemisia dracunculus

FROM ITS NATIVE habitat of western Asia, where it is used with great enthusiasm by Georgian cooks, tarragon reached Europe with the Moors. As classic French cooking developed in the 17th century, it became a key flavoring. Its finest uses are still in the French tradition.

LEAVES
Tarragon's aroma develops in cooking, but can easily overwhelm other flavors: use carefully, and it will enhance other herbs.

AROMA & TASTE
The aroma is warm and spicy, with notes of anise; the taste is refined, yet firm, with a light touch of pepper and anise, warm and subtle, but penetrating.

CULINARY USES
Indispensable in *fines herbes*, tarragon flavors many classic French sauces — *béarnaise, ravigote, gribiche, tartare.* It makes one of the best herb vinegars and lifts mustard to another realm. Use it with eggs, chicken, rabbit, crab, lobster, scallops, asparagus, leeks, avocado, and mushrooms, and in tomato salad.

Fresh tarragon is best but it freezes well. Use only French, not the coarse-flavored Russian tarragon (*A. dracunculoides*).

For recipes, see pages 66, 90, 101, 105, 106, 125.

SOUTHERNWOOD

Artemisia abrotanus

ONE OF THE PRETTIEST aromatic small shrubs, southernwood, as its name implies, is native to the Middle East and southern Europe. It has a delicate scent of lemon and pine, with a medicinal background note. Use the young, tender shoots for cooking.

LEAVES
A fine bitter citrus flavoring for beef, pork, salmon, eel, and mackerel. Use with lemon thyme or balm to bring out the citrus element.

MUGWORT

Artemisia vulgaris

MUGWORT GROWS WILD through much of Europe and Asia. It aids the digestion of fat and is used primarily with pork, duck, and goose — in Germany, where it is widely cultivated, it is known as "goose herb." In Asia it is boiled or stir-fried.

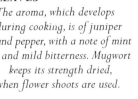

LEAVES
The aroma, which develops during cooking, is of juniper and pepper, with a note of mint and mild bitterness. Mugwort keeps its strength dried, when flower shoots are used.

CALAMINT
Calamintha species

CALAMINT, OR MOUNTAIN BALM, grows wild in southern Europe and western Asia. Used for perfumes, pharmaceuticals, and in the production of liqueurs, it also has a reputation as a culinary herb in southern European cuisines. Its sweetly peppery and minty aroma deserves more attention from cooks elsewhere.

AROMA & TASTE
The whole herb is aromatic with notes of thyme, mint, camphor, and a suggestion of tangerine peel; the taste is moderately pungent, warm, and lightly peppery.

CULINARY USES
Treat calamint like a milder form of mint. Use it to flavor grilled fish, roast lamb, all forms of game, and in marinades, stuffings, or sauces. Its peppery notes combine well with eggplant, all types of beans, lentils, mushrooms, potatoes, and tomatoes.

Calamint is used dried for making tea; for cooking, use fresh shoots and young leaves.

For recipes, see pages 97, 114.

COMMON CALAMINT
C. officinalis
Calamint is an attractive perennial with lilac-purple flowers and velvety leaves.

GARDEN CALAMINT
C. grandiflora
This has pink flowers and larger slightly drooping leaves; there is also a variegated form.

CATMINT AND CATNIP
Nepeta species

WIDELY GROWN IN temperate regions, these pretty herbs are sweetly aromatic with notes of mint and camphor. Cooks can benefit from their slightly sharp flavor in salads, soups, sauces, with pork and duck.

CATMINT
N. racemosa
Catmint's leaves are downy, and the blue or the lavender flowers are long lasting.

CATNIP
N. cataria
Catnip is usually more aromatic than catmint; it has white or pink flowers.

For recipes, see pages 97, 139.

MOUNTAIN MINT
Pycnanthemum pilosum

NATIVE TO North America, mountain mint is a graceful plant with pink flowers, reddish stems, and narrow leaves that look something like savory.

LEAVES
Use the shoots and young leaves of mountain mint as a mint substitute, but sparingly. It has a distinctive mint aroma with a strong menthol component. The taste is minty with bitter notes.

SUMMER AND WINTER SAVORY
Satureja species

BEFORE SPICES REACHED Europe, savory was one of the strongest flavorings available. Native to the Caucasus and eastern Mediterranean, it has been used for 2,000 years. Its warm peppery aroma is appreciated around the Black Sea and in southern Europe, notably in Provence. Summer and winter savory are interchangeable, but adjust the quantities.

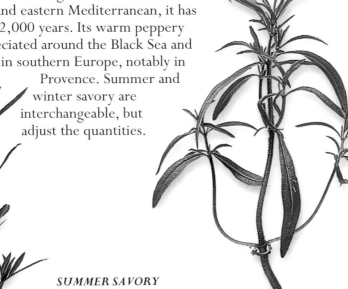

SUMMER SAVORY
S. hortensis
An annual garden herb with soft gray-green leaves, summer savory enhances vegetables. Try it with eggplant, onions, peas, peppers, tomatoes, and beans.

WINTER SAVORY
S. montana
A perennial evergreen with rather tough leaves. Use sprigs and remove before serving.

AROMA & TASTE
Summer savory is the more subtle, pleasantly piquant with similarities to marjoram and thyme. The aroma of winter savory is more assertive, with an additional note of pine, the taste more penetrating.

CULINARY USES
Known as the bean herb (for its anti-flatulent properties as well as its aromatic character), summer savory suits green and fava beans; winter savory is more satisfying with the haricot tribe. Use summer savory in salads and with mackerel, carp, pike, chicken, and squab. Winter savory suits meat and game dishes, stews and gratins.

Use both types fresh.

For recipes, see pages 91, 94, 102, 106, 109, 116.

THYME-LEAF SAVORY
Satureja thymbra

NATIVE TO SARDINIA, Crete, and Greece, this creeping plant does not survive cold climates. Its aroma has notes of thyme, mint, and savory; the taste is closer to savory with a pleasant bite.

LEAVES
Thyme-leaf savory can be used in the same way as winter savory or thyme, in slow-cooked soups and stews, especially with meat or game.

MICROMERIA
Micromeria species

MICROMERIA IS native to southern Europe. It is warmly aromatic, with notes of thyme and savory. In Balkan cooking it is used like thyme; the Italians use it in pasta sauces and omelets, with fresh cheeses and poultry.

EMPEROR'S MINT
Micromeria thymifolia has the finest aroma but is not available in all countries; emperor's mint is coarser with the taste of bitterish mint.

HYSSOP
Hyssopus officinalis

THIS COMPACT DECORATIVE perennial is native to southern Europe, southern Russia, and North Africa. It is hardy, easy to grow, and, as an evergreen, is available to the cook year-round. It has a long history as a culinary, cleansing, and medicinal herb; its volatile oil is used in the preparation of liqueurs.

LEAVES
An attractive plant and good addition to the culinary repertoire. Fresh or dried leaves can be used for tea.

FLOWERS
The bright blue, pink, or white aromatic flowers can be used in cooking. They also attract bees.

AROMA & TASTE
Hyssop's aroma is difficult to define: camphor refined by savory and lavender, with a hint of rosemary. Its slightly bitter taste combines elements of these with slight mintiness.

CULINARY USES
The flavor is strong, so use hyssop sparingly. It combines well with parsley, chervil, bay, thyme, and mint, and is good with rich meats — pork, lamb, kid, venison. Chopped young leaves and flowers go well in green salads, with the cabbage family, and with dishes of beans and lentils. It also has an affinity for plums and apricots.

Hyssop dries well; harvest it when just in flower.

For recipes, see pages 105, 115, 116, 120.

AGASTACHE
Agastache species

THE AGASTACHES ARE native to North America. Anise hyssop is starting to find some popularity in Europe now, and this erect showy herb, with its spikes of lilac flowers, is a handsome addition to a sunny part of the garden and well worth the cook's attention.

ANISE HYSSOP
A. foeniculum
The light green leaves give an elusive anise note when used in salads. In North America it is grown for honey.

MEXICAN HYSSOP
A. mexicana
Sometimes called giant hyssop, this variety grows wild in Mexico, where the leaves and flowers are used to make tea.

AROMA & TASTE
Both leaves and flowers of anise hyssop smell lightly of anise and licorice; the taste is sweetly anise. Mexican hyssop is minty.

CULINARY USES
Anise hyssop can be used to flavor fish and shellfish dishes and sauces to serve with them. It combines well with green beans, tomatoes, zucchini, and young beets. Add just before the end of cooking. Its sweetness also makes it a good companion to fruit; try a little in place of the tarragon in the pear and raspberry salad (page 113). Add finely chopped leaves to cream cheese and garnish with the flowers.

Anise hyssop can be frozen but is not worth drying.

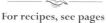

For recipes, see pages 79, 115, 116.

BERGAMOT
Monarda didyma

POPULARLY CALLED bergamot, bee balm, Oswego tea, or horsemint, the genus is named for Nicolas Monardes, a Spanish physician whose *Joyfull Newes out of the Newe Founde Worlde* (translated Frampton, 1577) was the first American herbal. This stately perennial, with its bright mopheads of flowers, is native to North America. In the 18th century seeds were taken to Britain.

FLOWERS
The purple, red, or pink flowers are the most fragrant part of the plant, and add a dramatic splash of color to a green or fruit salad.

BERGAMOT TEA
Early settlers along the north-eastern seaboard of America found the Indians made a tea from the plant and adopted the habit.

AROMA & TASTE
Flowers and leaves have a distinctive citrus aroma and taste, ranging from lemon to orange according to the variety.

CULINARY USES
Add leaves to duck and chicken dishes, and use them in omelets, salsas, and sauces. Use the flowers in salads and with fruit: the citrus flavor has a particular affinity for melon, strawberries, papaya, and kiwifruit. Bergamot tea is good, and if you add a couple of flowerheads to a pot of Indian tea, it will have a fine scented aroma and flavor.

Use fresh flowers and leaves for cooking; dried may be used for tea.

For recipes, see pages 79, 115, 129.

LEMON BALM
Melissa officinalis

A PERENNIAL, native to southern Europe, lemon balm is not a showy plant. It has the characteristic square stems of the mint family, crinkled light green leaves, and small white flowers.

VARIEGATED BALM
M.o. **'Aurea'**
More compact and less hardy than ordinary balm, this makes a brilliant splash in the border and the salad bowl.

PLAIN-LEAF BALM
Balm makes one of the best tisanes, but use a generous amount because it loses its aroma in hot water. Dried leaves can be used for tea.

AROMA & TASTE
Crushed leaves yield a fresh and persistent lemon aroma; the flavor is sweet and subtly lemon-scented with a note of mint.

CULINARY USES
Balm is excellent with poultry and fish, in stuffings, marinades, and sauces, and makes a delicate herb butter and fine vinegar. Tear young leaves for salads. They team well with virtually any steamed or sautéed vegetable, with rice, and cracked wheat. Use shredded leaves with lemon zest as a garnish. Add balm to custards, ice creams, desserts, cakes.

Fresh is best but it freezes well for 2–3 months.

For recipes, see pages 93, 124, 129.

SCENTED GERANIUMS
Pelargonium species

SCENTED GERANIUMS reached Europe in the 17th century from the Cape of Good Hope. In the 19th century the French perfume industry discovered their oil in place of attar of roses and geranium growing boomed.

P. crispum 'Variegatum'
An upright shrubby plant with crimped leaves that are freshly lemon-scented.

FLOWERS
The flowers of scented geraniums are small and have virtually no smell.

P. 'Graveolens'
Rose-scented with a hint of spice, reminiscent of rose water or Turkish delight.

P. crispum 'Prince of Orange'
This low, compact geranium has a sweet orange scent.

P. 'Attar of Roses'
Aptly named, this has a sweet concentrated rose perfume and pale pink flowers. Use a leaf or two to scent a jar of sugar, as you would a vanilla bean.

AROMA & TASTE
There are some 200 aromatic varieties. Some have fruit aromas – lemon, orange, apple; some are spicy – clove, cinnamon, nutmeg; others have the scent of flowers or woodland – rose, pine. Rose and lemon are the two most widely used in the kitchen.

CULINARY USES
Infuse the leaves in cream, milk, wine, or syrup and use the liquid to flavor ices, custards, other desserts and cakes. Leaves put in the bottom of a cake tin will impart a subtle flavor. Add leaves for the last few minutes when making jam or jelly.

Use fresh leaves.

For recipes, see pages 124, 125.

COSTMARY
Tanacetum balsamita

"THESE PLANTS grow everywhere in gardens, and are cherished for their sweet floures and leaves," wrote Gerard in 1633. Today costmary is something of a rarity. It can look straggly, but has the advantage that it persists into winter.

LEAVES
The aroma and taste are of mint and balsam. Use sparingly in salads, vegetable soups, and purées and with roast chicken.

For a recipe, see page 96.

RUE
Ruta graveolens

NATIVE TO southern Europe, rue is a handsome evergreen with soft bluish-green leaves and bright yellow flowers. A bitter herb with an assertive aroma, the taste is spicy and sharp. Use with caution; large amounts can be toxic.

VARIEGATED RUE
Variegated is used as plain. Add rue to a mix of basil, mint, oregano, parsley, savory, and thyme to use in place of salt.

PLAIN-LEAF RUE
Use a leaf or two in salads, herb stuffings, vegetable soups, cheese dishes; also in marinades for game and herb vinegars.

For recipes, see pages 115, 134.

SWEET CICELY

Myrrhis odorata

INDIGENOUS TO northern Europe, sweet cicely, or anise chervil, is a graceful perennial with light green fernlike leaves. Slow growing, it will eventually reach 3ft (1m) in height and width. It blooms early, bearing white flowers in spring, and by midsummer has umbrella-like seedheads.

AROMA & TASTE
The leaves and seeds have a musky aroma and taste of anise with a note of lovage and a decided sweetness.

CULINARY USES
Leaves and ripe seeds can flavor cakes, fruit pies, cream cheese, or sweet cream sauces. The leaves give a subtle flavor to omelets, salads, or a clear Asian-style chicken soup, and bring out the sweetness of root vegetables and squash. Stir some chopped leaves into a purée of carrots, parsnips, or pumpkin.

Use as soon as possible after cutting as the leaves wilt quickly.

For recipes, see pages 83, 116, 120, 122.

SEEDS
These taste almost better than the leaves. Green seeds add a spicy note and nutty texture to salads; use ripe, black seeds for desserts.

LEAVES
A natural sweetener, the leaves reduce the tartness of other foods. The flavor has an affinity for apricots, peaches, and nectarines.

WOODRUFF

Galium odoratum

THIS PRETTY creeping plant's scent is faint when fresh, but cutting releases the heady aroma of new-mown hay. This remains when the sprigs are dried or frozen and is readily transferred to liquids.

LEAVES
Woodruff has an affinity for melon, pears, and apples. Add to grape or apple juice. A syrup is used to flavor desserts and cakes. Infuse in marinades and dressings. Use sparingly.

For recipes, see pages 125, 129.

MARSH MALLOW

Althaea officinalis

ONCE GROWN widely for its medicinal and culinary properties, marsh mallow is now rather neglected. An attractive perennial, it has a light musky smell and sweet taste.

LEAVES AND FLOWERS
Use in salads; they go well with fennel. Leaves are stir-fried or steamed. Marsh mallow sweets were once made from the roots.

SEEDS
Add these to marinades and salad dressings and to breads.

For a recipe, see page 115.

ASIAN HERBS

During the last ten years several Asian herbs have become popular in the West, with the spread of Thai restaurants and the development of East-West and Pacific Rim cuisines. Each year a few more plants arrive in specialty nurseries – there was a noticeable increase after travel began again to Vietnam, where fresh herbs are part of every meal. Many deserve to be more widely known.

SANSHO

Zanthoxylum piperitum

IN JAPAN *kinome*, sprigs of young leaves of the sansho, or prickly ash tree, are picked as an herb. Only used fresh, their season is limited and they are not easy to find in the West.

DRIED BERRIES
The ground powder is sprinkled on fatty foods, and is one of the seven ingredients of shichimi, *used as a table condiment.*

LEAVES
Crush leaves lightly to release the aroma; try them in clear soups and with salads.

AROMA & TASTE
The taste is delicately minty.

CULINARY USES
Kinome sprigs are used as a garnish for soups, tofu, seafood, and grilled meats. Add chopped leaves to dressings for Japanese and Western salads, especially of raw root vegetables. Sansho berries are ground to a tangy powder that has a slightly numbing sensation in the mouth.

The sprigs keep for a few days in the refrigerator.

PERILLA

Perilla frutescens

NATIVE TO CHINA, perilla has long been grown in Japan. Also called *shiso* and beefsteak plant (the red variety), leaves are sometimes sold in Asian stores, and the sprouts in supermarkets. It also grows easily in the garden or in a pot.

RED PERILLA
In Japan this is mostly pickled (sold in vacuum packs). Use big fresh leaves to wrap poultry or fish for steaming or braising.

GREEN PERILLA
A useful and attractive addition to the herb garden; shred leaves for soups and salads, fresh white cheeses, and herb butter.

AROMA & TASTE
Green perilla is sweetly aromatic, with notes of anise, cinnamon, and lemon. Red is faintly musty with notes of cilantro leaf and cinnamon.

CULINARY USES
Leaves and seeds are eaten with *sushi* and *sashimi* (perilla counteracts parasites in raw fish). Chopped leaves make an excellent flavoring for rice and pasta, salmon, sea bass, and turbot. Fry whole leaves in tempura batter.

For recipes, see pages 86, 114.

LEMONGRASS
Cymbopogon citratus

THIS TALL PALE green grass is native to tropical
Asia. It is now cultivated in Australia and Florida
and has become widely available. It will flourish
in cooler climates if it is overwintered indoors.
The lemon rind perfume, with a hint of
sweetness, gives a fresh subtle fragrance to
cooking from Indonesia to Vietnam. It blends
harmoniously with chili, garlic, and shallots,
with cilantro, and Asian varieties of basil.

STALKS
*Remove outer leaves and use
only the bulbous bottom parts
of the stalks; the rest is very
fibrous. Very freshly cut stems
show purplish rings.*

AROMA & TASTE
The clean lemon aroma is
echoed in the taste, a blend
of lemon and lime, subtle
but sustained.

CULINARY USES
Use the bottom part of the
stalks; crush them to
put in marinades or the
steaming water for fish and
chicken. Coarsely chop
and pound for Thai curry
pastes. Finely slice for
soups and stir-fries.

Lemongrass enhances the
flavor of fish, seafood,
chicken, beef, and pork;
also broccoli, cabbage,
eggplants, and mushrooms.

Keep for 2–3 weeks in the
refrigerator or 2–3 months
in the freezer. Dried, as
stalks or powdered, it lacks
the clean taste of fresh.

**For recipes, see pages
60, 72, 88.**

KAFFIR LIME LEAVES
Citrus hystrix

THE LEAVES AND RIND of the fruit of this evergreen
tree are responsible for the light tangy edge to
Thai and Indonesian dishes. In the West it
has become easier to buy fresh leaves (and
sometimes the wrinkled knobbly fruits) as
well as dried leaves and rind, or pickled
rind, from Asian shops.

LEAVES
*These grow as two on a single
petiole; use fresh leaves when
possible, dried are a less
fragrant substitute.*

AROMA & TASTE
Kaffir lime has a floral-
citrus aroma, similar
to lemon verbena, delicate
yet assertive. The rind
is strongly citrus and
slightly bitter.

CULINARY USES
Both zest and leaves are
used in soups, curries,
and stir-fries. Soak
dried strips of rind in warm
water first. Shredded
leaves are sometimes used
as a garnish, but they are
tough to chew on. I prefer
to cook with whole leaves
and remove them. Add a
couple of leaves to a
Western stew or casserole
instead of bay for an elusive
citrus flavor.

Leaves keep for 2–3 weeks
in the refrigerator and
freeze well.

**For recipes, see
pages 60, 72.**

CURRY LEAVES
Murraya koenigii

THE LEAVES – called *meetha neem* in India – of a small tree that grows wild throughout the subcontinent but is also cultivated in Indian gardens for its attractive foliage and for culinary purposes. Curry leaves are a daily essential in southern Indian and Sri Lankan cooking. Buy them, preferably fresh, from Indian stores and some supermarkets.

LEAVES
Put a spray of leaves into Western dishes to give a light curry note. Dried have little flavor; it takes 2–3 times as many to give the aroma and flavor of a fresh sprig.

AROMA & TASTE
When bruised, curry leaves give off a currylike scent with a citrus note. The taste is warm, bitterish, and pleasant.

CULINARY USES
In southern India and Sri Lanka fresh sprigs are fried with spices, put into simmering meat, vegetable, and fish dishes (to be removed at serving), chopped into fresh chutneys, and ground for spice mixtures. They are an essential ingredient of south Indian curry powder. Try them in the aromatic oil – the *tadka* – that flavors the lentil dish on page 105.

Keep leaves in the refrigerator for a week or two, or freeze.

For a recipe, see page 88.

CHINESE BOXTHORN
Lycium barbarum

ALSO CALLED matrimony vine, boxthorn is grown for food in Asia and as an ornamental in Europe. The leaves are peppery and mintlike.

LEAVES
In China boxthorn is used as a potherb and for soup, traditionally with pork or pig's liver. Try adding the leaves to Western soups and stews, but cook them briefly.

BERRIES
These have a licorice-like flavor when ripe; use them in meat stews. Dried berries are sold as wolfberries.

SPICE BUSH
Elscholtzia stauntonii

THIS SMALL temperate-climate shrub, also called mint bush, has toothed leaves that turn red in autumn and purplish pink flowers. Its sweet aroma of caraway and anise is echoed in the taste, with hints of mint and lemon.

LEAVES
Stir the chopped leaves into mashed potato, vegetable purées, or a cream sauce for game; you can also add them to a green salad.

MITSUBA
Cryptotaenia japonica

IN JAPAN, MITSUBA leaves and stems are used to season soups, fish and vegetable dishes, and savory custards. It is cooked very briefly to preserve its flavor. Small bundles of stalks are often tied in knots just below the leaves and fried for tempura or used as a garnish.

LEAVES
The flavor of mitsuba has elements of parsley and angelica, a hint of clove, and something of the sharpness of sorrel; it is distinctive, restrained, and agreeable.

For a recipe, see
page 86.

RAO RAM
Polygonum odoratum

VARIOUSLY CALLED Vietnamese cilantro, parsley, or mint, rao ram has an intensified aroma of cilantro with peppery citrus notes. In Southeast Asia it is usually eaten raw as a salad or herb accompaniment, but it remains aromatic when lightly cooked. A great discovery, and well worth seeking out. Use like cilantro.

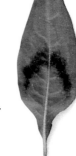

LEAVES
P. odoratum has oval leaves with purplish markings; the related P. foetidum with longer, plain green leaves and a nasty rank aroma and taste should be avoided.

For recipes, see pages
94, 97, 112.

PANDANUS
Pandanus odoratissimus

THE MUSKY new-mown hay aroma of pandanus (screwpine) is a common flavoring for Southeast Asian desserts. Infuse leaves in cream or milk to give Western puddings a subtly exotic fragrance.

LEAVES
Combined with coconut, the flavor of pandanus is delicious. Leaves go into pilafs; Indian kewra essence, which is distilled from the flowers, scents syrups and sweets.

For a recipe, see
page 88.

VAP CA
Houttuynia cordata

A PERENNIAL water-loving plant, much used on herb platters in Vietnam and neighboring countries. Crushed leaves have a mild lemony yet acrid aroma; the taste is pleasantly sourish.

LEAVES
Use chopped leaves to flavor simmered or braised dishes of fish or pork. Shred leaves into a clear Asian-style soup. Some varieties have a rank smell; test before buying.

HERBS FROM THE AMERICAS

Many Mediterranean and other European herbs were taken to the Americas by colonists. Now some of the indigenous herbs are making their way onto the world market as demand has grown with greater awareness of the culinary traditions of Mexico and South America. Some of these are unique to the Americas, but others are also found in tropical Asia.

CULENTRO
Eryngium foetidum

ALSO CALLED *cilentro* and *cilantrón,* this herb is used in Caribbean and Central American cooking and in Southeast Asia (where it is *ngó gai* to the Vietnamese). It is related to cilantro, but more pungent. Buy it from Thai stores.

AROMA & TASTE
The fetid element of cilantro is more pronounced in culentro; the taste is earthy and pungent.

CULINARY USES
Use the leaves like cilantro but with restraint. In Mexico and the Caribbean it flavors stews, soups, and salsas. In Southeast Asia it goes into curries and soups. Combine with lemongrass and mint to give soups and sauces a sourish flavor.

LEAVES
The long serrated leaves are prickly and tough; dried leaves are said to keep their flavor better in long cooking.

EPAZOTE
Chenopodium ambrosioides

CONSIDERED PRIMARILY a Mexican herb, its use spreads across the northern countries of South America. It combines well with chilies, cilantro, and oregano – the main flavorings of the region.

AROMA & TASTE
Epazote smells sharply camphorous; the taste is pungent, bitterish, and citrusy. It is restricted in some countries.

CULINARY USES
In Mexico it is essential for black bean dishes and for *quesadillas* (cheese-filled tortillas). Young leaves are cooked as potherbs; it flavors pork, crab cakes, fish, corn, and squash.

For recipes, see pages 68, 87.

LEAVES
Epazote grows easily and is often found as a weed in North America, but in cooler conditions it is less aromatic.

MEXICAN OREGANO
Lippia, Poliomintha, and other genera

THE NAME OREGANO is given to several unrelated plants that smell and taste somewhat like oregano. *Poliomintha longiflora* has narrow leaves similar to summer savory; other oreganos belong to the Monarda genus; Cuban and Puerto Rican oreganos are succulents (see page 17). Use with chilies and other herbs to flavor meats, beans, and vegetable stews, or try them instead of Mediterranean oregano in other dishes.

LIPPIA GRAVEOLENS
The most common Mexican oregano, belonging to the lemon verbena family. It is sweet smelling, with a hint of clove, but can taste harsh and bitterish when raw.

MINT MARIGOLD
Tagetes lucida

ALSO CALLED winter tarragon, the Mexican name *yerbanis* seems more accurate for the aroma is delicately aniselike with a hint of mint. Mint-scented marigold leaves and flowers are excellent in salads, the leaves enhance fish and shellfish, eggs, tomatoes, and avocados. Use them for vinegar and add chopped leaves to sauces.

LEAVES
Both the leaves and golden marigold flowers, in late summer, are scented. Used extensively in the Southwest.

SASSAFRAS
Sassafras albidum

AN ORNAMENTAL North American tree with aromatic leaves, formerly used medicinally and as a tea, the roots to flavor root beer and the oil to cure toothache. It is now known that safrole, a constituent of sassafras oil, is a carcinogen. Safrole is not present in the dried leaves.

FILE POWDER
Filé powder may be made only of dried sassafras leaves or may have dried thyme, oregano, or bay added to it.

AROMA & TASTE
The young leaves are dried and ground to make filé powder, which smells and tastes sourish, rather like lemony sorrel with notes of tea. The flavors are enhanced by brief heating.

CULINARY USES
Filé powder is a key ingredient, probably taken over from the local Indians, in the cooking of Louisiana, where it is used to flavor and thicken gumbos.

Gumbo, a Cajun soup, contains vegetables, fish, or seafood, or a variety of meats and is served with rice. The filé powder is added at the end of cooking. Try it in similar soups and stews.

SALAD HERBS

A salad without herbs tends to be bland and dull. Those shown here are mostly used whole, mixed generously with other leaves; a tablespoon or two of chopped herbs will flavor a salad. Be sure to balance the pungent with the milder herbs.

ARUGULA

Eruca vesicaria ssp. *sativa*

KNOWN IN North America by its Italian name, arugula is called rocket in parts of Europe. It is native to western Asia and southern Europe. Popular until the 18th century, when it almost disappeared in northern Europe, it now enjoys a well-deserved revival.

LEAVES
Arugula has toothed leaves and small white or yellow flowers. It is easy to grow, especially in partial shade.

TURKISH ARUGULA
Bunias orientalis
Grows wild in parts of Asia; it has a sharper flavor, rather like horseradish.

AROMA & TASTE
Arugula has a warm, peppery smell; the taste is pleasantly pungent. The piquant edible flowers have a faint orange aroma.

CULINARY USES
Whole leaves can be added to any composed salad, or make a fine flavored salad on their own, especially with a nut oil dressing. Arugula and new potato salad is good. Shredded leaves can be used for herb butter or in an herb dressing for pasta.

Use fresh; do not freeze.

For recipes, see pages 83, 113, 115.

SORREL

Rumex acetosa

GARDEN SORREL GROWS easily throughout the temperate zones. French sorrel prefers the drier climate of the Mediterranean. Both are high in vitamin C and folic acid, the latter giving the sour taste.

FRENCH SORREL
Rumex scutatus
French or buckler leaf sorrel is finer and more succulent than garden sorrel, with a lemony note.

AROMA & TASTE
Sorrel has little aroma but a tart sharp taste, with a hint of lemon.

CULINARY USES
Use leaves whole or shredded. It makes a fine soup with a sour, refreshing tang. Sorrel purée balances the richness of duck and pork, goes well with eggs, and, finished with cream or egg yolk, makes a good sauce for fish.

Use fresh, although cooked sorrel can be frozen.

For recipes, see pages 72, 78, 90, 108, 116, 139.

WOOD SORREL
Oxalis acetosella
Although unrelated, this has a similar taste and is refreshing in salads and summer drinks.

GARDEN SORREL
Use young leaves in salads; treat older ones like spinach. Cooked in butter, it combines with spinach or chard.

WINTER PURSLANE

Montia perfoliata

ALSO KNOWN AS claytonia, this hardy but delicate-looking annual has a mild fresh flavor. It is a useful salad herb all year round but is especially welcome in autumn and winter.

LEAVES
Both winter and summer purslane combine well with fava beans, beets, and new potatoes.

SUMMER PURSLANE

Portulaca oleracea

THE FLESHY LEAVES are crunchy and refreshing. A standard ingredient of Middle Eastern *fattoush* and Provençal *mesclun*, purslane has an affinity for chervil, burnet, and the cresses.

LEAVES
Produces several crops if shoots are harvested regularly. Bundles can often be bought in Middle Eastern and Greek stores.

For recipes, see pages
83, 112, 115.

DANDELION

Taraxacum officinale

USE THE BITTER but appetizing young leaves in spring salads. They are also good combined with new potatoes, pieces of crisp bacon, and a garlicky or walnut oil dressing.

LEAVES
These can be made more tender by blanching them during growth (covering them to exclude light); they look similar to curly endive.

For recipes, see pages
113, 115.

SALAD BURNET

Sanguisorba minor

BURNET IS COOL and astringent, reminiscent of cucumber. Use young leaves for green salads and in sauces, in mixtures of *fines herbes*, and to blend into cream cheese.

LEAVES
Burnet is seldom found for sale as a cut herb, but it makes an attractive garden plant, often lasting well into winter. Always use fresh leaves.

For recipes, see pages
79, 84, 91, 115, 136.

EDIBLE FLOWERS

Flowers are being rediscovered as food, a fragrant link to the past, when dozens were gathered for the kitchen. Violet wine, flower puddings, lavender conserve, and pickled marigolds were not culinary exotica but part of the normal diet, at least of the well-to-do.

MARIGOLDS

Calendula officinalis and *Tagetes patula*

IN ANCIENT TIMES the pot marigold was valued for its edible qualities in India, the Arab lands, and by the Greeks. Parkinson noted its "pretty strong and resinous sweet sent," that leaves and flowers were used as a potherb, and the flowers for possets, broths, and drinks.

POT MARIGOLD
C. officinalis
Marigold petals can be dried in a very low oven and then ground.

FRENCH MARIGOLD
T. patula
The flavor of these petals, dried, blends well with cinnamon and cloves.

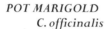

AROMA & TASTE
Both marigolds have a musky aroma and a lightly bitter, musky taste.

CULINARY USES
Dried marigold petals have long been used in Europe as poor man's saffron to color rice and other dishes. In Russian Georgia, they prefer French marigolds; they are an essential flavoring, used in spice mixtures and with chili pepper, garlic, and walnuts. Fresh petals can be used in salads and desserts after removing the bitter white heel. See also page 43.

For a recipe, see page 115.

NASTURTIUMS

Tropaeolum majus

THE CONQUISTADORES brought nasturtiums from Peru to Europe in the 16th century. They combine well with parsley, tarragon, burnet, and chives. The seeds can be pickled.

SEEDS
Soak seeds in salted water for 24 hours; strain. Boil enough white wine vinegar to cover them. Cool and pour over the seeds. Leave for 6 months.

FLOWERS
These make a fine vinegar with some white peppercorns and mace (see page 136).

LEAVES
Add young leaves, shredded or whole, to a mushroom and bean salad (see page 112), with a dash of pastis in the dressing.

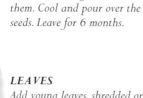

AROMA & TASTE
Leaves and flowers taste peppery, rather like watercress. The flowers are sweeter.

CULINARY USES
Young leaves are good in sandwiches and salads. The flowers look pretty in green salads. Scatter them over new potatoes or Great Northern beans or stir them into a risotto. Sliced leaves and flowers put into a vegetable soup for the last few minutes give an agreeable pepperiness.

For recipes, see pages 112, 113, 115.

CLASSIC DISHES

This section features traditional dishes from many countries, showing the great variety in the use of herbs in different cultures. Most of these recipes use fresh herbs, alone or in combination with other flavorings. Coriander (cilantro) is used in nearly all the major cuisines, parsley throughout the Western ones. Other herbs, such as tarragon and lemongrass, are more particularly associated with one area or tradition.

All the recipes serve 4, unless otherwise indicated.

SOUPE AU PISTOU

Vegetable soup with pistou

This substantial soup from Provence is served with pistou, the local version of Genoese pesto. The vegetables may vary, but squash or pumpkin, some root vegetables, and beans are always used. The soup is almost better reheated, but make the pistou at the last moment. Serves 6.

INGREDIENTS

7 cups (2 liters) water
1 large onion, chopped
3 carrots, diced
2 small turnips, diced
4 potatoes, diced
½lb (250g) winter squash or pumpkin, peeled and diced
¾ cup (150g) Great Northern beans, soaked and boiled for 10–15 minutes
bouquet garni made up of bay leaves and sprigs of parsley, thyme, and sage, tied together
¼lb (150g) green beans, cut into short lengths
3 zucchini, diced or quartered
1 cup (75g) short macaroni or pasta shells
2 medium tomatoes, peeled and chopped
salt and black pepper

Pistou
large handful of basil leaves
3 garlic cloves
coarse salt and black pepper
½ cup (60g) freshly grated Parmesan
approximately ½ cup (120ml) olive oil

PREPARATION

1 Bring the water, lightly salted, to a boil and add the onion, carrots, turnips, potatoes, squash, soaked beans, and bouquet garni. Reduce the heat and simmer, covered, for about 30 minutes, or until the vegetables are just beginning to soften.
2 Add the green beans, zucchini, macaroni, and tomatoes and simmer for 15 minutes longer, until the pasta is cooked but still *al dente*.
3 To prepare the pistou, tear the basil leaves and pound them with the garlic, salt, and pepper in a mortar. Add the Parmesan gradually, alternating it with spoonfuls of olive oil, to make a thick paste. You may find this easier to mix with a large fork than with a pestle. Continue until all the cheese and oil have been amalgamated.
4 Season before serving and remove the bouquet garni. The pistou should not be heated, but served separately as an accompaniment. Stir well as the oil has a tendency to separate from the rest of the sauce.
KCal 495 P 16g C 54g S 154mg SFA 5g UFA 18g

Green beans

Bouquet garni

Great Northern beans

Squash

Potatoes

Turnips

Carrots

Onion

Tomatoes

Macaroni

Zucchini

Basil

Garlic

Salt

Black pepper

Parmesan

Olive oil

GRAVLAX

Scandinavian salmon marinated with dill

An elegant dish that is simple to prepare. The dill imparts a delicate flavor to the salmon and the slight sweetness of the mustard sauce balances it well. Mackerel and trout can be prepared in the same way, but salt them only for the shorter suggested time. Serves 8–10.

INGREDIENTS

4lb (2kg) salmon, preferably a center cut
½ cup (100g) sea salt
⅓ cup (75g) sugar
1 tbsp white peppercorns, crushed
2 large bunches of dill, chopped
Mustard Sauce
3 tbsp Dijon mustard
½ tsp dry mustard
1 tbsp sugar
3 tbsp lemon juice
⅓ cup (75ml) sunflower or other flavorless oil
4 tbsp chopped dill

PREPARATION

1 Scrape away all the scales from the salmon with the back of a knife, but leave the skin on. Slit the fish open along the backbone and remove it. Check both fillets for bones and remove them. You may find a pair of tweezers useful for this.

2 Combine the salt with the sugar and white pepper and rub the mixture well into the flesh of each piece of salmon.

3 Scatter a third of the dill over the bottom of a shallow dish just large enough to hold the salmon. Put in one piece of fish, skin side down, and cover this with another third of the dill. Put the other half of the salmon on top, flesh side down, and strew over the rest of the dill.

4 Cover the dish with plastic wrap, then place a weighted board on top and leave in the refrigerator for at least 36, and preferably 48, hours. Turn the fish once during this time and baste it with any brine that collects in the dish.

5 Just before serving the salmon, combine the two mustards with the sugar, lemon juice, and oil to make the sauce. Whisk together thoroughly and, when they are well blended, stir in the dill.

6 Drain the fish and scrape off the dill and spices, then slice it thin on the diagonal and serve with the mustard sauce and bread or new potatoes. The salmon will keep in the refrigerator for up to a week, although it will start to dry out.

KCal 441 P 35g C 13g S 1100mg SFA 4g UFA 21g

Dill

White peppercorns

Sugar

Sea salt

Salmon

Dijon
mustard

Dry
mustard

Lemon
juice

Sunflower
oil

TURKISH ZUCCHINI PANCAKES

These simple pancakes, called *mücver*, are always a great success whether served hot as a vegetable course or part of a vegetarian meal, or cold for a picnic or buffet. The Turks sometimes use finely diced eggplant, and a little green pepper and tomato instead of zucchini, to make the pancakes.

INGREDIENTS

6–7 tbsp olive or sunflower oil
2 large onions, grated
3 zucchini, grated
¼lb (100g) white cheese, such as feta,
grated or crumbled
5 tbsp chopped dill
5 tbsp chopped flat-leaf parsley
4 tbsp sifted all-purpose flour
3 eggs
salt and black pepper
sprigs of dill or parsley, to garnish

PREPARATION

1 Heat a tablespoon of oil in a skillet and sauté the onion until golden.

2 Squeeze the excess moisture from the grated zucchini by pressing it in a colander or sieve or squeezing it in handfuls. Then add the grated zucchini to the pan and cook over a high heat for 2–3 minutes. Put to one side.

3 Whisk the cheese, dill, parsley, flour, and eggs together in a large bowl. Season, but check on the saltiness of the cheese before adding more salt.

4 Pour the contents of the skillet into the cheese and eggs and mix well.

5 Wipe out the pan and add enough of the remaining oil to shallow fry the pancakes. When the oil is hot, drop in tablespoons of the mixture one by one to make small pancakes. Leave room for them to spread a little. Cook until the pancakes are golden brown on both sides. Do not try to turn them until the undersides are thoroughly browned or they may fall apart.

6 Blot the pancakes on paper towels and serve them garnished with a few sprigs of dill or parsley. The pancakes can be eaten hot, warm, or cold. A tomato salad or a bowl of garlic-flavored yogurt makes a good accompaniment.

KCal 426 P 14g C 20g S 428mg SFA 8g UFA 22g

Dill

Feta
cheese

Zucchini

Onions

Olive
oil

Flat-leaf parsley

Flour

Eggs

Salt

Black pepper

TABBOULEH
Bulgur wheat and herb salad

A traditional Lebanese salad, also popular in neighboring countries. Proportions of bulgur wheat to herbs and tomatoes vary, but it is essential that the wheat play only a background role. The salad should be predominantly green and red, with specks of cream, and taste vibrantly of parsley and lemon. Tabbouleh is served as part of *mezze* (hors d'oeuvres) in the Middle East.

INGREDIENTS
⅓ cup (60g) bulgur wheat
4–5 scallions, finely chopped
1lb (500g) ripe tomatoes, peeled, seeded, and chopped,
with the juice reserved
2 large bunches of flat-leaf parsley, total weight
approximately ¾lb (350g), leaves chopped
5 tbsp chopped mint leaves
½ cup olive oil
juice of 1 lemon, or more to taste
salt and black pepper
½ tsp ground allspice
1 head lettuce, preferably romaine or other firm variety

PREPARATION

1 Soak the bulgur wheat in a bowl of cold water for 20 minutes, until soft and swollen. You can check whether it is sufficiently tender by nibbling a grain or two. If not, leave for a few minutes longer. Drain in a sieve and press out any excess water.
2 Add the scallions and tomatoes, with as much of their juice as possible. Stir in the parsley and mint. The best way to mix the salad is with your hands.
3 Make a dressing by whisking together the oil, lemon juice, salt, pepper, and allspice – the salad should have a tart, lemony flavor. Stir the dressing into the tabbouleh and let stand for 30 minutes or so at room temperature before serving, so that the flavors have time to blend.
4 To serve, line a platter with the lettuce leaves and use them to scoop up the tabbouleh, which is piled in the center of the dish. An assortment of raw vegetables, such as scallions, radishes, carrots, and cucumbers cut into wedge-shaped batons, makes a good accompaniment.
KCal 397 P 7g C 21g S 47mg SFA 4g UFA 25g

Mint

Flat-leaf
parsley

Tomatoes

Scallions

Bulgur wheat

Olive
oil

Lemon juice

Salt

Black
pepper

Ground
allspice

Lettuce

SALADS

The judicious addition of fresh herb leaves can transform a few simple ingredients into a memorable salad. Depending on their characteristics, you can use herbs to add a mild, subtle flavor or a more dominant note, but always take care to balance the tastes and textures of the salad.

MANGO, MINT, AND SHRIMP SALAD

Refreshing and light, the mint, lime juice, and garam masala give a sharp, clean taste to the creamy dressing. Serve as a first course.
See page 115 for recipe.

RED PEPPER SALAD WITH OLIVES AND ANCHOVIES

Cilantro is usually associated with Asian or South American food, but its pungent, lemony taste combines well with the traditional Mediterranean flavors of roasted red peppers, olives, and anchovies.
See page 115 for recipe.

DAIKON AND KIWIFRUIT SALAD

Inspired by Japanese cuisine, this salad combines the spicy-sweet flavor of basil or perilla leaves with the crisp texture of the radish and refreshing kiwifruit.
See page 114 for recipe.

FAVA BEAN SALAD WITH PROSCIUTTO

A combination of summer beans, prosciutto, and sweet tomatoes is finished with a generous scattering of fresh marjoram.
See page 114 for recipe.

HERB AND FLOWER SALAD

Refreshing in color and flavor, this delicate tangle of green leafy herbs is garnished with violas and nasturtiums to make a tempting display.
See page 115 for recipe.

THAI VEGETABLE CURRY

All the ingredients for this curry can be found in Thai and Asian stores, many in supermarkets. If you have to use substitutes, the curry will lack subtlety, although the flavor will be good. You can use fewer chilies, but this quantity gives depth of flavor rather than excessive heat.

INGREDIENTS

1 cup (250ml) thick coconut milk
2 cups (500ml) thin coconut milk
½lb (200g) green beans, cut into short lengths
3 zucchini, thickly sliced and quartered
½lb (200g) broccoli florets
8oz (250g) canned bamboo shoots, sliced
6 kaffir lime leaves (if unavailable, use lemongrass or grated lime or lemon rind)
10 small white eggplants, quartered
3–4 tbsp Thai fish sauce

Green Curry Paste

2 lemongrass stalks, lower part only, thinly sliced
6 thin slices galangal (if unavailable, use fresh ginger)
1 tsp chopped kaffir lime peel
2 tbsp chopped cilantro root (if unavailable, use leaves)
5 shallots, chopped
3 garlic cloves, crushed
1 tsp shrimp paste (or a dash of fish sauce)
½ tsp coriander seeds, roasted
½ tsp cumin seeds, roasted
10–15 birdseye or other small green chilies, or to taste
¾oz (20g) Thai or sweet basil leaves
To garnish: holy basil leaves and 1 large green chili

PREPARATION

1 Mix ½ cup (100g) creamed coconut with 1 cup (175ml) water for thick milk, and ⅓ cup (75g) with 1½ cups (400ml) water for thin. Or, if using canned milk, chill the cans first to separate thick and thin.
2 Pound the curry paste ingredients with a mortar and pestle or blend in a processor until smooth.
3 Heat the thick coconut milk in a wok and stir in the curry paste. Cook for about 10 minutes, stirring frequently, until the oil starts to seep out.
4 Add the green beans and zucchini and toss for a few minutes. Pour in the thin coconut milk and bring to a boil, then add the broccoli, bamboo shoots, and kaffir lime leaves and cook until the beans have almost softened. Add the eggplants and simmer until soft, 5–8 minutes longer.
5 Season with fish sauce and remove from the heat. Discard the kaffir lime leaves. Scatter over the torn basil and finely sliced green chili. Serve with rice.
KCal 417 P 13g C 19g S 580mg SFA 27g UFA 4g

Fish sauce

White eggplants

Kaffir lime leaves

Bamboo shoots

Broccoli

Zucchini

Green beans

Creamed coconut

Garlic

Cumin seeds

Green
chili

Kaffir
lime peel

Cilantro
root

Shallots

Shrimp
paste

Coriander
seeds

Birdseye
chilies

Basil

Galangal

Holy
basil

Lemongrass

JAMBALAYA

This highly seasoned rice dish is always started with that trinity of Louisiana ingredients, onion, celery, and green pepper, and invariably uses dried herbs. Jambalaya varies according to the cook and the ingredients at hand, but a mixture of seafood and meat is common.

INGREDIENTS

2 tbsp butter or 2 tbsp sunflower oil
1 large skinless chicken breast, cubed
½lb (200g) ham, preferably smoked, chopped
1 onion, chopped
2 celery sticks, sliced
1 green pepper, seeded and diced
2 scallions, chopped
3 garlic cloves, chopped
2 bay leaves, crushed
1½ tsp dried thyme
1 tsp dried oregano
5 fresh sage leaves, shredded
4 tbsp chopped flat-leaf parsley
3 large tomatoes, peeled and chopped
2½ cups (600ml) chicken stock or water
salt
½ tsp black pepper
½ tsp cayenne
1¼ cups (200g) long-grain rice
20 large shrimp, cooked and peeled

PREPARATION

1 Heat the butter or oil in a large heavy pan, add the chicken and ham, and cook over low heat for 5–6 minutes, stirring frequently, until browned.
2 Add the onion, celery, and green pepper and let them start to brown before adding the scallions, garlic, bay leaves, thyme, oregano, sage, and half the parsley. Cook for 5 minutes, stirring and scraping the bottom of the pan if necessary.
3 Put in the tomatoes and stock, and season with salt, if necessary, and black pepper and cayenne.
4 When the liquid comes to a boil, stir in the rice. Let it come back to a boil, cover, and reduce the heat. Simmer for 20–25 minutes, until the rice is tender but still has a bite.
5 Distribute the shrimp evenly through the mixture. Simmer, uncovered, for 5–10 minutes, until they are heated through. It will probably help to stir with a wooden fork during this last stage of the cooking, to keep the rice grains separate.
6 Check the seasoning and stir in the remaining parsley. Serve hot.
KCal 430 P 31g C 50g S 829mg SFA 6g UFA 6g

Sage leaves

Dried oregano

Bay leaves

Garlic

Scallions

Green pepper

Celery

Onion

Butter

Smoked ham

Chicken breast

Cayenne

Salt

Black
pepper

Chicken stock

Long-grain
rice

Shrimp

Tomatoes

Flat-leaf
parsley

ried
yme

MEAT DISHES

Herbs such as rosemary, oregano, and thyme, which are high in aromatic oils and can withstand heat, are the best to use with meat, when high temperatures or long cooking are needed. Simple grilled meats can be quickly finished with a *persillade*, a mixture of parsley and garlic, or an herb butter, see pages 135–36.

PORK NOISETTES WITH FENNEL

Although it is more often associated with fish, fennel is an excellent herb for flavoring braised pork.
See page 101 for recipe.

GRILLED STEAK WITH BEARNAISE SAUCE

This classic French combination is easy to prepare as long as you do not rush the sauce making. Tarragon, an essential herb for many French sauces, gives béarnaise a fine, pure flavor.
See page 101 for recipe.

SALTIMBOCCA ALLA ROMANA

A simple dish that can be made in a matter of minutes. The combination of veal, prosciutto, and sage is a great Italian favorite.
See page 100 for recipe.

ARISTA ALLA FIORENTINA

*Rosemary is the traditional
Italian herb for pork. In this
dish it is combined with
garlic and cloves to season
a finely flavored roast.*
See page 100 for recipe.

LAMB KLEFTIKO

*A Greek recipe that gives
extra succulence to the meat.
The pungency of the oregano
is mellowed in these slowly
cooked bundles of lean lamb.*
See page 100 for recipe.

CHICKEN WITH TARRAGON

Chicken with tarragon is a classic of French bourgeois cooking. Simple to prepare, it has a delicate yet distinct flavor of tarragon. Serve the chicken with rice or boiled potatoes, spinach, glazed carrots, snow peas, or young fresh fava beans. The leftover stock will make a flavorful soup. Serves 6.

INGREDIENTS

2 tbsp butter
3 carrots, finely sliced
2 onions, finely sliced
1 celery stalk, finely sliced
7 cups (1¾ liters) chicken stock
1 chicken, weighing approximately 3lb (1.5kg)
1 cup (250ml) dry white wine
small bunch of tarragon
salt and black pepper
1 egg yolk
½ cup (100ml) crème fraîche or light cream
1 tsp flour

PREPARATION

1 Heat the butter in a pan large enough to hold the chicken. Add the carrots, onions, and celery and cook gently, with the lid on, until they are softened, but do not let them brown.
2 In a separate pan, heat the stock until warm.
3 Add the chicken to the vegetables, placing it breast up, and pour over the stock and wine. There should be enough liquid to cover the chicken – if necessary, add a little water. Bring to a boil over medium heat and skim off any surface scum.
4 Reserve 3 tablespoons of tarragon leaves for the sauce and add the rest to the pan. Season with salt and pepper.
5 Cover tightly and let the chicken poach for about an hour. (The stock should just shudder, not bubble.) Check to see if the bird is cooked by inserting the point of a knife where the thigh joins the body – there should be no trace of blood. When ready, remove the chicken, being careful to drain it well when you lift it from the pan, carve it, and keep warm while you make the sauce.
6 Strain the stock, pour 1⅔ cups (400ml) into a pan and boil to reduce it by half. Beat the egg yolk with the crème fraîche and flour. Remove the stock from the heat and stir in the egg mixture to make a smooth, creamy sauce. Then add the reserved, finely chopped, tarragon leaves. Serve the sauce separately.
KCal 287 P 25g C 11g S 157mg SFA 7g UFA 6g

Chicken stock

Celery

Onions

Carrots

Butter

Chicken

Tarragon

Salt

Black pepper

Crème fraîche

Egg yolk

Flour

Dry white wine

DUCK WITH MOLE VERDE

The appetizing green color of the sauce, or *mole verde*, in this classic Mexican dish comes from the blend of pumpkin seeds, herbs, and tomatillos, a light green tart fruit in a papery husk. The dish is based on a recipe in Diana Kennedy's *The Cuisines of Mexico*.

Lettuce

Onion

Garlic

Serrano chilies

Tomatillos

Pumpkin seeds

Duck breasts

INGREDIENTS

4 duck breasts
Mole Verde
1 cup (100g) hulled pumpkin seeds
6 tomatillos, fresh or canned
4 serrano chilies, chopped and seeded
2 garlic cloves, crushed
1 small onion, chopped
6 romaine lettuce leaves, torn
bunch of watercress or radish tops
3 tbsp chopped cilantro
leaves from 3 sprigs fresh epazote, or 1 tbsp dried
good pinch of ground cumin
black pepper
2 tbsp sunflower or peanut oil
1 cup (250ml) chicken stock

PREPARATION

1 To make the mole verde, dry-roast the pumpkin seeds in a skillet for 4–5 minutes, stirring so that they do not color too much or burn. Set aside to cool, then grind them.

2 Blend the tomatillos in a food processor with the chilies, garlic, onion, lettuce leaves, watercress, cilantro, epazote, cumin, and pepper. (If you are using fresh tomatillos, first remove the husks and cut the flesh into chunks.)

3 Heat the oil in a pan and cook the sauce over high heat so that it thickens, stirring from time to time. It will take about 5 minutes. Set aside.

4 Stir the pumpkin seeds into the stock, or purée the two together in a blender, and add to the sauce.

5 Heat a heavy skillet and put in the duck breasts, skin side down. Cook them in their own fat for 10 minutes, turn once, and cook for 5 more minutes. They should remain slightly pink.

6 While the duck is cooking, very gently heat the sauce, making sure that it does not boil or it will lose its greenness. Let it barely simmer for 15 minutes, stirring regularly.

7 Lift the duck from the pan, remove all the fat, and slice the meat. Spoon the sauce onto a serving platter, arrange the slices of duck on top, and serve with tortillas.

KCal 431 P 37g C 10g S 191mg SFA 4g UFA 22g

Watercress

Cilantro

Epazote

Ground cumin

Black pepper

Chicken stock

Peanut oil

RECIPES

This part of the book contains a selection of dishes from around the world in which herbs play an important part. Sometimes their use is completely traditional, but many of the recipes include unusual varieties or use familiar herbs in unexpected ways. The different flavors that can be produced will, I hope, encourage you to develop your own ideas into successful dishes.

All the recipes serve 4, unless otherwise indicated.

SOUPS, APPETIZERS, AND EGG DISHES

Herbs whet the appetite. In the Middle East a bowl of aromatic leaves and salad greens always accompanies the assortment of dips, salads, little pies, and vegetable dishes that make up the *mezze* at the beginning of a meal. Herb soups such as chervil or cucumber and borage make an elegant first course; more hearty combinations with vegetables can make a meal in themselves.

SCALLOP AND HERB SOUP

I first encountered this soup at the Thai Cooking School at the Oriental Hotel in Bangkok, and this recipe is based on theirs. Reduce the number of chilies if you prefer your food less fiery. Extra lime juice can replace the tamarind if necessary.

INGREDIENTS

10oz (300g) scallops
3½ cups (800ml) canned coconut milk
2 stalks lemongrass, lower part only, finely sliced
4 shallots, finely chopped
5 kaffir lime leaves
3 tbsp fish sauce
1 tsp brown sugar
2 tbsp lime juice
2 tsp tamarind paste
6 red or green birdseye chilies, seeded and pounded
chopped cilantro leaves and a few shreds from a large chili, to garnish

PREPARATION

1 Bay scallops can be used whole, but if you have a larger variety, cut them in half or thirds horizontally.
2 Bring one cup (250ml) of the coconut milk almost to a boil. Add the lemongrass, shallots, and kaffir lime leaves.
3 Stir in the fish sauce, sugar, lime juice, and tamarind paste, making sure that the latter dissolves in the liquid. Add the birdseye chilies.
4 Pour in the remaining coconut milk. When it is hot, put in the scallops and simmer for 4–5 minutes. Remove from the heat, discard the kaffir lime leaves, and serve garnished with the cilantro and chili shreds.
KCal 383 P 21g C 14g S 621mg SFA 23g UFA 3g

ELIZABETH RAPER'S HERB SOUP

This recipe is based on one in Miss Raper's "receipt" book, written 1756–1770. During this time she married Dr. William Grant, an ancestor of Duncan Grant, the painter. Her receipt book remained in the family and was published in 1924. Serves 6.

INGREDIENTS

2–3 handfuls of sorrel leaves
2–3 handfuls of chervil
handful of beet leaves
2 handfuls of parsley leaves
3–4 young leeks or scallions
¼ head green cabbage
1 lettuce
handful of spinach leaves
8 tbsp (125g) butter
4 cups (1 liter) good beef stock
4–6 thin slices bread, crusts removed
salt and black pepper

PREPARATION

1 Chop all the herbs and vegetables very fine. Melt the butter in a large saucepan and sauté them for 3–4 minutes.
2 Pour in the stock, add the slices of bread, and season with salt and pepper. Bring the soup gently to a boil, then simmer for about 15 minutes, or until the bread disintegrates and thickens the soup.
KCal 267 P 7g C 18g S 433mg SFA 12g UFA 6g

VARIATIONS

Miss Raper notes that peas may be added at the same time as the stock and bread, and that if you want to make a meatless version, the amount of butter should be increased by half and the beef stock replaced by water.

CUCUMBER SOUP WITH BORAGE

A simple chilled summer soup. The borage and cucumber complement each other to give it a delicate yet sustained flavor. If you like buttermilk, try it instead of yogurt, and sour cream or crème fraîche can replace the cream.

INGREDIENTS

2 cucumbers, peeled, seeded, and chopped
5 scallions, chopped
large handful of borage leaves
1¼ cups (300ml) cold chicken stock or consommé
1¼ cups (300ml) plain yogurt
⅔ cup (150ml) heavy cream
salt and black pepper
pinch of cayenne
a few drops of lemon juice, optional
borage flowers to garnish, optional

PREPARATION

1 Blend together the cucumbers, scallions, and most of the borage leaves to make a purée. Add a ladleful or two of the stock to thin the mixture and blend again.
2 Transfer the purée to a large serving bowl or soup tureen.
3 Whisk together the rest of the stock with the yogurt and cream and stir into the cucumber purée. Season with salt, pepper, and cayenne and, if you want a sharper flavor, a little lemon juice. Refrigerate the soup until thoroughly chilled.
4 Before serving, shred the rest of the borage leaves and scatter them over the soup. If you have any borage flowers, they look very pretty floating on the surface.
KCal 148 P 7g C 12g S 110mg SFA 5g UFA 3g

PARSLEY SOUP

This vivid green soup has a fine parsley flavor. It can be eaten hot or cold. Serves 6.

INGREDIENTS

2 very large bunches of flat-leaf parsley
1 tbsp virgin olive oil
6 scallions, thinly sliced
2 garlic cloves, chopped
3¾ cups (900ml) vegetable or chicken stock
1 large potato, thinly sliced
salt and black pepper
1¼ cups (300ml) heavy cream or plain yogurt
lemon zest and chopped parsley or mint,
to garnish

PREPARATION

1 Strip the leaves from the parsley. Heat the oil and cook the scallions, garlic, and parsley stems slowly for about 15 minutes, until soft.
2 Add the stock, potato, and seasoning. Simmer for about 20 minutes, until the potato is soft enough to be crushed with the back of a spoon.
3 Meanwhile, bring a large pan of water to a boil. Add the parsley and, as soon as the water returns to a boil, drain and refresh it under cold water to retain the bright green color.
4 Purée together the parsley leaves and soup base, then pass through a sieve. Check the seasoning.
5 If the soup is to be served hot, stir in the cream and reheat gently. If serving the soup chilled, let it cool completely, then stir in the cream. Garnish with lemon zest and parsley or mint.
KCal 169 P 4g C 10g S 47mg SFA 6g UFA 6g

LOVAGE SOUP

This recipe is from Bohemia and is based on a recipe given to me by Zdena Lancellotti, wife of Angelo Lancellotti, whose salad recipes appear on page 113. Serves 6.

INGREDIENTS

3 medium potatoes, diced
6 cups (1½ liters) water, lightly salted
2 onions, chopped
2 tbsp sunflower oil or butter
2 tbsp paprika
handful of lovage leaves, chopped
salt and black pepper
1 egg
2–3 tbsp semolina

PREPARATION

1 Add the potatoes to the water and bring to a gentle boil. Meanwhile, sauté the onions in the oil until golden. Add the paprika and stir well.
2 Once the paprika has darkened, add the onion mixture to the potatoes as they cook. Then add most of the lovage. When the potatoes are cooked, blend and return the soup to the pan. Check the seasoning, adding salt and pepper to taste.
3 Break the egg into a bowl, whisk lightly, and add enough semolina to make a firm paste, rubbing the two together as if you were making pastry. Roll it between your fingers into tiny balls or batons, and when all are ready, drop them into the soup.
4 Gently heat the soup through for 5–10 minutes, then serve, garnished with the remaining lovage.
KCal 172 P 5g C 24g S 156mg SFA 1g UFA 5g

CHERVIL SOUP

Chervil's light green, lacy leaves produce a pale, delicately colored soup, which is popular in many north European countries. If you cannot buy big bunches of chervil, it is easy to grow in the garden. Serves 4–6.

INGREDIENTS

4 tbsp butter
2 shallots, chopped
2 tbsp all-purpose flour
4 cups (1 liter) chicken or vegetable stock
2 egg yolks
6 tbsp cream
3½oz (100g) chervil leaves and thin stems,
finely chopped
salt and black pepper

PREPARATION

1 Melt the butter in a saucepan and soften the shallots for a minute or two, then stir in the flour to form a roux. Keep stirring and cook for 3–4 minutes longer without letting it brown.
2 Warm the stock and add it gradually, stirring constantly, until the mixture is smooth and starts to thicken. Simmer for 20 minutes, stirring from time to time.
3 Beat the egg yolks and mix in the cream and chervil, reserving a little chervil for a garnish.
4 Stir a ladleful of warm soup into the chervil and egg mixture. Pour this all into the pan. Stir well.
5 Heat the soup without letting it boil, or it will curdle. Season with salt and pepper and serve at once, scattering a little chervil over each bowl.
KCal 218 P 4g C 8g S 137mg SFA 11g UFA 6g

PANZANELLA

This peasant dish from Tuscany is currently enjoying a vogue in Italian restaurants. Its success depends on using good-quality bread and the best olive oil. Do not be tempted to use packaged bread — it won't work.

INGREDIENTS

*4 thick slices stale country bread, such as
pane toscano
4 ripe tomatoes
1 red onion, thinly sliced
1 cucumber, seeded and cubed
handful of basil, using a mixture of green and purple
leaves if possible
leaves from a sprig of mint
handful of parsley leaves, preferably flat-leaf
2–3 tbsp red wine vinegar
6–8 tbsp (approximately 100ml) virgin olive oil
salt and black pepper*

PREPARATION

1 Cut off and discard the crusts from the bread and soak it in cold water for 10 minutes. Squeeze the bread dry, then tear it into bite-sized pieces.
2 Core and slice the tomatoes, being careful to reserve any of their juices.
3 Put the bread in a salad bowl with the tomatoes, including their juice, and the onion and cucumber. Tear the basil leaves into small pieces and roughly chop the mint and parsley. Add them to the bread and vegetables.
4 Whisk together the vinegar and oil to make a dressing, and season with salt and pepper.
5 Turn the salad in the dressing, mixing it well so that all the pieces of bread are coated with the oil and vinegar. Check the seasoning.
6 Let stand for an hour or so before serving so that the flavors blend.
KCal 377 P 6g C 28g S 226mg SFA 4g UFA 22g

CEVICHE OF SCALLOPS

*Ceviche comes originally from Peru, where it is usually
served accompanied by thick slices of boiled
sweet potato and corn. Any firm-fleshed fish can be
prepared in this way; the lime or lemon juice marinade
"cooks" the fish. Cilantro is the herb used in
South America, but dill is also very good with
delicately flavored seafood such as scallops.
Serves 4—6.*

INGREDIENTS

1½lb (750g) scallops
juice of 5—6 limes or lemons
2—3 green chilies, seeded and finely sliced
3 large tomatoes, skinned, deseeded and diced
1 small red onion, finely chopped
6 tbsp chopped dill
⅓ cup (90ml) olive oil
salt
1 avocado (plus a little lime or lemon juice) and
a few sprigs of dill, to garnish

PREPARATION

1 If you are using large scallops, slice them
horizontally, but leave small bay scallops whole.
2 Put them in a dish and add enough lime juice to
cover. Turn the scallops so that all sides are coated
with juice, and cover the dish with plastic wrap or
a plate. Marinate in the refrigerator for 3—4
hours. The lime juice brings about a chemical
change similar to that produced by heat, and the
scallops will become opaque.
3 Drain and discard the juice from the scallops
and combine them with the chilies, tomatoes,
onion, chopped dill, and olive oil. Season with
a little salt.
4 Return the dish to the refrigerator until ready
to serve. Then peel and slice the avocado, brushing
it with lime juice to prevent it from discoloring,
and use it to garnish the scallops, along with the
sprigs of dill.
KCal 500 P 46g C 12g S 545mg SFA 5g UFA 23g

VARIATIONS

Seville orange juice or a mixture of regular orange
juice and lemon juice can be used as an alternative
marinade. Try it with a mixture of salmon and one
of the white fish such as brill, monkfish, sea bass,
or halibut.

Cut the fish into ½—¾in (1—2cm) cubes and
remove any bones. For 1½lb (750g) fish you will
need the juice of 4—5 Seville oranges, or combine
the juice of one regular orange with that of 4—5
lemons or limes. Replace the dill with cilantro.

Red
onion

Tomatoes

Green
chilies

Lime juice

Scallops

Dill

Olive oil

Salt

Avocado

SASHA'S GUACAMOLE

This Mexican dish, a favorite of my daughter, can be served as a side dish or dip, or as a sauce for grilled fish.

INGREDIENTS

5 ripe but firm tomatoes, seeded and finely cubed
1½ medium onions, finely chopped
4 tbsp finely chopped cilantro
2–3 tsp seeded, chopped jalapeño chili
salt and black pepper
juice of 1 lime or, if not available, lemon
2 ripe avocados

PREPARATION

1 Put the tomatoes, onions, cilantro, and chili in a serving bowl, season to taste, and mix in the lime juice. Cover and refrigerate for 30 minutes to give the flavors time to blend. Up to this point the guacamole can be made several hours in advance.
2 At the last moment, peel and mash the avocados and stir into the mixture. Serve with tortilla chips.
KCal 130 P 3g C 8g S 15mg SFA 2g UFA 7g

BAKED EGGS WITH SORREL

INGREDIENTS

3½oz (100g) sorrel leaves
1 tbsp butter, plus extra for pan
½ cup (125ml) heavy cream
1 or 2 eggs per person
black pepper

PREPARATION

1 Heat the oven to 350°F/180°C. Place a shallow pan of water (bain-marie) inside to warm.
2 Roll up and shred the sorrel leaves. Cook them in the butter until they have melted into a purée.
3 Generously butter four ovenproof ramekins. Put a layer of sorrel in the bottom of each, then add a tablespoon of cream. Break in one or two eggs and drizzle with a second tablespoon of cream.
4 Set the ramekins in the bain-marie and bake for 8–10 minutes, until the eggs are cooked to your liking. Season with black pepper and serve with bread or toast.
KCal 230 P 7g C 1g S 101mg SFA 12g UFA 8g

MINT AND PARSLEY FRITTATA

Italian frittate are quite thick, unlike French omelets, and can be served cut into wedges. They are good eaten hot or at room temperature. Serves 4–6.

INGREDIENTS

8 eggs
salt and black pepper
½ cup (60g) grated romano cheese
1½ tbsp fresh bread crumbs
2 tbsp chopped mint
2 tbsp chopped flat-leaf parsley
2–3 tbsp olive oil

PREPARATION

1 Beat the eggs, season with salt and pepper, and mix in the cheese, bread crumbs, and herbs.
2 Heat the oil in a large skillet and add the egg mixture. Tilt the pan and lift the sides of the frittata as it cooks, so that the runny center is distributed around the edge of the pan.
3 When the frittata is almost set, and looks golden brown underneath as you lift the edge, turn it over to cook the top for 2–3 minutes. An easy way is to invert a plate over the pan, remove the frittata, then slide it back in. Alternatively, put the pan under a preheated broiler for 2 minutes to set the top.
KCal 310 P 18g C 3g S 252mg SFA 7g UFA 16g

CHIVE FLOWER OMELET

This recipe is based on one from the Shaker village of North Union in Ohio, published in The Best of Shaker Cooking *by Amy Bess Miller and Persis Fuller (1970). Serves 2.*

INGREDIENTS

4 large eggs
1 tbsp chopped parsley
1 tbsp chopped chives
1 tbsp chopped chervil
1 tsp chopped tarragon
salt and black pepper
2 tbsp butter
handful of chive flowers

PREPARATION

1 Beat the eggs lightly, just enough to blend the whites and yolks. Stir in the herb leaves and season.
2 Heat a heavy skillet and, when very hot, add the butter. Swirl it around so that the melted butter covers the base and sides. Pour in the egg mixture, shake vigorously, and stir with a fork, lifting the mixture at the edges of the pan so that it cooks evenly. This takes only a minute.
3 Scatter the chive flowers over half the omelet, fold it over, and slide onto a warm serving dish.
KCal 296 P 16g C 1g S 480mg SFA 12g UFA 10g

LATKES WITH SALMON

These potato pancakes make an attractive dish for a first course or for a light meal accompanied by a salad.

INGREDIENTS

¾lb (375g) salmon fillet
1 bunch chives or 5–6 small scallions
2 eggs
4 tbsp all-purpose flour
2 tbsp chopped basil, preferably lemon basil
2 tbsp chopped bergamot leaves
salt and black pepper
3 large potatoes, each weighing about ½lb (250g)
sunflower or light vegetable oil, for frying

Herb Sauce
½ cucumber, seeded, grated, and the liquid
squeezed out
scant ½ cup (100ml) sour cream or crème fraîche
4 tbsp mixed chopped herbs, such as parsley, basil,
bergamot, anise hyssop, or marjoram

PREPARATION

1 If you have a thick salmon fillet, cut it lengthwise to give pieces about ½in (1cm) thick, then cut those to make 16 pieces.
2 Chop the chives into ¾in (2cm) lengths. If using scallions, cut them in half lengthwise first.
3 Whisk the eggs lightly, mix with the flour and herbs, and season with salt and pepper. Peel and grate the potatoes and combine them with the egg mixture quickly so they do not turn brown.
4 Heat a few tablespoons of oil in a skillet. Put in 1 tablespoon of potato mixture, flatten it with a spoon, and cook for 1½ minutes. Press a piece of salmon on top firmly, and cook for 30 seconds.
5 Turn once and cook for up to 1 minute, until slightly colored. Drain well on paper towels and keep warm. You can cook 2–3 latkes at a time.
6 To make the sauce, stir the cucumber into the sour cream and add the herbs. Serve the latkes with the sauce on the side.
KCal 556 P 30g C 41g S 205mg SFA 7g UFA 21g

HERB PANCAKES WITH SMOKED TROUT

Illustrated on page 80. Serves 6.

INGREDIENTS

¾ cup (100g) all-purpose flour
pinch of salt
1 egg
1 egg yolk
1 cup (250ml) milk, or milk and water,
preferably carbonated
3–4 tbsp sunflower oil
4–5 tbsp coarsely chopped mixed herbs, such as chervil,
parsley, dill or anise, salad burnet, a little young
angelica, a little fenugreek, caraway, lemon verbena
6 smoked trout fillets

Horseradish Sauce
½ cup (125g) cream cheese or ricotta
scant ½ cup (100ml) sour cream
1 tsp grated horseradish, or to taste

PREPARATION

1 Sift the flour with the salt. Whisk the eggs with the milk, add 1 tablespoon of oil, then whisk in the flour. Beat until smooth, like a light cream. Add a little more milk or water if necessary. Strain and add the herbs. Let rest for at least 30 minutes.
2 Make the sauce by mixing the cream cheese, sour cream, and horseradish. Cover and chill.
3 Remove any bones in the trout using tweezers.
4 To make the pancakes, heat a 7in (18cm) skillet (preferably nonstick) and brush it lightly with oil. Ladle in a little batter and quickly tilt the pan to spread it evenly over the bottom. When the pancake begins to curl, flip it over with a narrow spatula, or toss it. The second side takes much less time. Slide it out onto paper towels and cover with another sheet. Brush the pan with oil again and make the next pancake. Stack them as you go.
5 To serve, place a trout fillet on each pancake, fold in half, and serve the sauce separately.
KCal 657 P 25g C 16g S 924mg SFA 17g UFA 34g

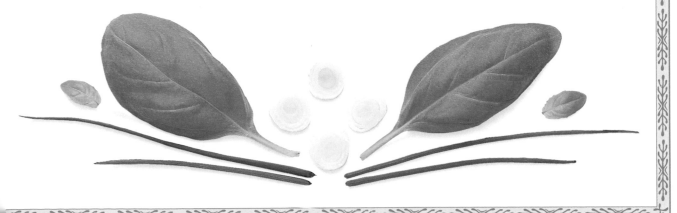

*Herb Pancakes
with Smoked Trout
(see previous page)*

*Moroccan Fish
Tagine with
Chermoula
(see page 82)*

FISH AND SEAFOOD

Herbs can be used when poaching fish, in marinades and stuffings, and in many sauces used for cooking or served as an accompaniment. Many classic French sauces are flavored with herbs and make excellent partners for poached and grilled fish.

MOROCCAN FISH TAGINE WITH CHERMOULA

A tagine is a round, flat earthenware dish with a conical lid, and tagine is also the generic word for stews in Morocco. The preserved lemons give a salty sharpness to slow-cooked foods and also to salads. Illustrated on previous page. Serves 6.

INGREDIENTS

1 large or 2 medium sea bass, bream, or red snapper, weighing approximately 3lb (1.5kg), scaled and gutted
1 tbsp olive oil
2 garlic cloves, sliced
¼ tsp chili powder
¼ tsp ground ginger
½ tsp paprika
26oz (800g) canned chopped tomatoes, drained
salt
handful of green olives
Chermoula
3 garlic cloves, finely chopped
peel from a preserved lemon, chopped (see right)
large bunch of flat-leaf parsley, chopped
large bunch of cilantro, chopped
2 bay leaves
a few sprigs of thyme
1 tsp paprika
½ tsp ground cumin
¼ tsp chili powder, preferably Moroccan
juice of 1 lemon
6 tbsp olive oil

PREPARATION

1 First make the chermoula by combining all the ingredients to form a thick paste.
2 Slash the sides of the fish in a couple of places to help the heat penetrate evenly. Put it in a tagine or other ovenproof dish and rub well with chermoula, making sure there is some in the cavity and in the cuts. Spread the remaining chermoula under and over the fish. Let the flavors develop, preferably for several hours.
3 Heat the oil and lightly cook the garlic and spices. Add the tomatoes, sprinkle with salt, and simmer until the mixture has reduced and thickened. There must be enough to cover the fish.
4 Heat the oven to 400°F/200°C.
5 Pour the tomato sauce over the fish, and scatter the olives on top. Cover the dish, and bake for 40 minutes to 1 hour, depending on the size and number of fish.
6 Traditionally, the fish is served straight from the tagine. Alternatively, arrange it with the sauce on a serving platter. Accompany with rice if you wish.
KCal 357 P 32g C 6g S 485mg SFA 3g UFA 17g

To make Moroccan preserved lemons, wash 4–5 lemons well and cut into quarters, but not all the way through. Sprinkle coarse salt into the cuts, close the lemons, and put them in a large jar. Press down, put a weight on top, and close the jar. In a few days sufficient juices should be released to cover the lemons. If not, add more lemon juice. Let stand for a month. Use the skin, not the flesh.

SKATE SALAD

A quickly assembled first course or light meal.

INGREDIENTS

2 skate wings, weighing approximately 2lb (1kg)
6 cups (1½ liters) court bouillon (see right)
1 bunch of arugula or watercress, large stems removed
3½oz (100g) purslane or mâché
½ red pepper, cut into strips
1 yellow zucchini, cut into strips
½ cucumber, cut into strips
4 scallions, sliced in long, thin strips
½ tsp chopped fresh ginger
½ tsp nigella seed (also known as kalonji)
juice of 1 lime
2 tsp chili oil, or pepper flakes to taste
3 tbsp sunflower oil
1–2 tsp fish sauce
1–2 tsp light soy sauce
1 tbsp chopped cilantro
1 tbsp chopped sweet cicely

PREPARATION

1 Poach the skate wings for 12–15 minutes in the court bouillon. Strain and let cool, then lift the flesh from the bones in long strips.
2 Make a bed of salad herb leaves and arrange the vegetable strips and skate on top.
3 Mix a dressing from the ginger, nigella seed, lime juice, oils, fish sauce, and soy sauce. Spoon over. Strew the cilantro and sweet cicely on top.
KCal 277 P 27g C 5g S 422mg SFA 2g UFA 13g

To make court bouillon, bring to a boil 6 cups (1½ liters) water, ½ cup dry white wine, 1 sliced carrot, 2 quartered shallots, 1 lemon slice, 8 crushed black peppercorns, 1–2 tablespoons herbs (chosen from celery, dill, lovage, marjoram, parsley, savory, tarragon, thyme). Simmer for 30 minutes, strain, and use. Court bouillon can be frozen.

VARIATION

Other salad herbs may be used; balm, burnet, orache, and perilla would make good additions.

TUNA WITH SALSA CRUDA

Salsa cruda is a good summer sauce for fried or grilled fish, or for pasta, but it is worth making only if you have ripe, flavorful tomatoes.

INGREDIENTS

4 tuna steaks, each weighing about ½lb (250g)
2 tbsp olive oil
Marinade
2 bay leaves, crumbled
a few parsley stems
a few sprigs lemon balm or lemon thyme
salt and black pepper
2 tbsp olive oil
2 tbsp red wine vinegar
Salsa Cruda
1lb (500g) ripe tomatoes, peeled and diced
large handful of basil leaves, chopped
2 garlic cloves, finely chopped
1 red chili, seeded and finely chopped
⅓ cup (90ml) extra-virgin olive oil
salt and black pepper

PREPARATION

1 Put half the herbs for the marinade in a flat dish, just large enough to hold the fish in one layer. Rub the tuna steaks with salt and pepper and add them to the dish. Strew the remaining herbs on top. Pour over the oil and vinegar, cover, and marinate for 1–2 hours, turning once.
2 Combine the ingredients for the salsa cruda an hour or so before serving to allow the flavors to blend. Season and keep at room temperature.
3 Lift the steaks from the marinade and discard the herbs. Heat the oil in a heavy pan and cook the steaks for 3–4 minutes on each side, depending on their thickness. If you prefer to broil or barbecue the steaks, brush them with oil and cook under a preheated broiler or over hot coals for 8–10 minutes, turning once. Serve the salsa cruda in a bowl separately.
KCal 504 P 37g C 5g S 375mg SFA 6g UFA 29g

VARIATIONS

Other firm fish steaks such as swordfish, salmon, or mahi-mahi can be substituted for the tuna.

If you cannot get flavorful tomatoes, it would be better to serve the fish with salmoriglio, salsa verde, lovage and lime relish, or red pepper relish (for details of how to make them, see pages 138–39). Alternatively, make a quick dressing by blending together a big handful of flat-leaf parsley, 2 shallots, a tablespoon of Dijon mustard, the juice of a lemon, and ⅔ cup (150ml) olive oil.

BAKED MACKEREL WITH HERBS AND ORANGE SAUCE

This recipe is adapted from William Verral's A Complete System of Cookery, *published in 1759. Buy the fish whole, without having them cleaned, so that the bellies are still intact.*

INGREDIENTS

4 mackerel, each weighing about 1lb (500g)
small bunch of fennel
small bunch of salad burnet
small bunch of sweet basil
small bunch of parsley or chervil
small bunch of thyme
a few mint leaves
7 tbsp (100g) butter, softened
salt and black pepper
½ cup (125ml) dry white wine
2 oranges, to garnish
Orange Sauce
2 tbsp chopped shallot, or ½ shallot, ½ rocambole
½ cup (125ml) dry white wine or fish stock
juice of 2 oranges

PREPARATION

1 Lay the fish on its belly on a work surface and, with a small knife, cut along either side of the backbone to free the two fillets from the bone. Snip the backbone at the head and 1in (2–3cm) above the tail with a pair of scissors, then work it and the ribs free of the flesh, taking care not to pierce the belly. Pull out the backbone (see opposite). Some of the innards may come with it; remove the rest with your finger.
2 Bend back the head to widen the gill openings and take out the gills (see opposite). Wash the fish thoroughly and pat dry.
3 Heat the oven to 400°F/200°C.
4 Chop all the herb leaves and fine stems and combine them with the butter. Season with salt and pepper. Divide the herb butter among the cavities of the four fish (see opposite).
5 Arrange the fish side by side in a baking dish, belly side down, and pour the wine around them. Cover with foil and bake for 15 minutes.
6 Prepare the orange sauce by cooking the shallot in the wine until the liquid has reduced by two-thirds. Add the orange juice. Boil for 1–2 minutes.
7 Cut the two oranges into quarters. To serve, arrange the mackerel, backs uppermost, using the orange quarters to support them, and pour the hot sauce on top. A dish of couscous with mixed vegetables makes a good accompaniment.
KCal 590 P 27g C 21g S 317mg SFA 18g UFA 20g

CLEANING AND STUFFING MACKEREL

1 Holding the fish belly side down, carefully cut along either side of the backbone. Snip it free at the head and tail. Then work it and the ribs free of the flesh and pull out.

2 Bend back the head of the fish to enable you to put your finger and thumb into the gill opening. Pull out the gills, or cut them out with scissors, if necessary, and discard them.

3 Lay the mackerel on its belly and spoon the herb and butter stuffing into the cavity. Keep as neat a shape as possible so that you can easily stand the fish upright in the baking dish.

TEMPURA

*The success of this classic Japanese dish depends
on getting the batter right and on ensuring that the oil
is at the correct temperature for frying each batch of
food, especially the mitsuba and perilla leaves.
Once everything is prepared, it is very quick to
make. Mirin, used in the dipping sauce, is a syrupy,
rice-based wine, used only for cooking. Dashi
is a stock made from dried bonito and kelp. Both
can be found in Japanese stores.*

INGREDIENTS

*flour, for coating
8 large raw shrimp
1 medium or large onion
12 stalks mitsuba
4 scallops
4 fresh shiitake or commercial mushrooms, trimmed
8 perilla leaves
light vegetable oil, for frying*

Dipping Sauce

*4 tbsp mirin or sake
4 tbsp light soy sauce
1 cup (250ml) dashi
2 tsp grated fresh ginger
3 tbsp grated daikon (mooli) radish*

Batter

*2 egg yolks
2 cups (500ml) ice water
2 cups (250g) all-purpose flour, sifted*

PREPARATION

1 Tempura is best eaten as soon as it leaves the
pan, but if you want to serve everything at the
same time, heat the oven to 350°F/180°C to keep
the batches warm. Prepare a bowl of flour for
coating, a draining rack, and paper towels.
2 Peel the shrimp, leaving the tails on. Score them
across the underside 2–3 times and flatten their
backs slightly with the flat blade of a knife so that
they do not curl when fried.

3 Cut the onion across into 4 slices and separate the rings. Alternatively, push 4 toothpicks through the onion, from side to side, and cut between them to give 4 slices. Leave the toothpicks in place.
4 Tie the stalks of mitsuba together in bunches of 3, in a loose knot just below the leaves. Trim the stalks to the same length.
5 Make the dipping sauce by bringing the mirin, soy sauce, and dashi to a boil. Remove from the heat and stir in the ginger and radish. Keep warm.
6 Mix half the batter just before starting to fry; do not make the second batch until needed. It should not stand before using. Gently mix an egg yolk with half the water, then add half the flour. Stir very lightly with a fork or chopsticks; the mixture should remain lumpy with bits of dry flour in it. If you overmix, it will be heavy.
7 Heat about 2½in (6cm) oil in a wok or wide pan to 335°–350°F/170°–180°C. Test by dropping in a small amount of batter; if it sinks, then rises to the surface, the temperature is right.
8 Do not crowd the pan; fry a few pieces at a time, according to size. Dip the shellfish and vegetable pieces in the flour, shake off any excess, then coat them in batter and slide them into the oil. Turn frequently with long chopsticks or a slotted spoon for about 3 minutes, until the batter turns a light gold and the pieces rise to the surface.
9 Fry the herbs for about 1 minute. They should not be floured. Coat only the stalks, not the leaves, of the mitsuba in batter, and only the underside of the perilla leaves.
10 Drain all the food well and serve with the dipping sauce.
KCal 399 P 25g C 57g S 1407mg SFA 2g UFA 6g

SHRIMP WITH GREEN SAUCE

This sauce is Mexican, a simpler one than the mole verde on page 68. It is thickened by reduction of the liquid, not by pumpkin seeds, and has less complex flavors.

INGREDIENTS

2 tbsp sunflower or peanut oil
2lb (1kg) large or medium raw shrimp
Green Sauce
¾lb (400g) tomatillos, fresh or canned
3 serrano or jalapeño chilies
4 tbsp chopped cilantro leaves
2 tbsp chopped epazote leaves (fresh if possible)
½ tsp ground cumin
2 large lettuce leaves, shredded
½ small onion, chopped
1 garlic clove, chopped
scant 1 cup (200ml) chicken or vegetable stock
salt

PREPARATION

1 To make the sauce, remove husks from fresh tomatillos. Simmer in just enough water to cover until soft, about 10 minutes. If canned, drain them. Purée with the other sauce ingredients until almost smooth – it should still have some texture.
2 Heat the oil until very hot but not smoking. Add the sauce and cook, stirring constantly, for 3–4 minutes, until it thickens and darkens a little.
3 Broil the shrimp for 3–4 minutes, until they turn pink, or sauté them in a heavy nonstick pan over high heat for about 5 minutes, turning once. Serve with the warm sauce.
KCal 389 P 61g C 5g S 541mg SFA 2g UFA 10g

FISH BAKED IN A CILANTRO AND NUT SAUCE

This dish of Lebanese origin can be made with any firm white fish such as bream, cod, tilapia, sea bass, or snapper.

INGREDIENTS

1 cup (125g) walnut pieces
juice of 1 lemon
good pinch of salt
½ tsp red pepper flakes
about 7 cups (200g) cilantro leaves
3 garlic cloves
small onion
2 tbsp olive oil
4 fish fillets

PREPARATION

1 Grind the nuts coarsely in a food processor; the sauce should retain a crunchy texture. Add 6 tablespoons water and the lemon juice and blend briefly with the salt and pepper flakes.
2 Heat the oven to 350°F/180°C.
3 Chop together the cilantro, garlic, and onion, or use a food processor. Heat the oil and cook the cilantro mixture for a few minutes. Stir in the nuts. Simmer for 2–3 minutes. Check the seasoning.
4 Spread a little of the sauce over the bottom of an ovenproof dish just big enough to hold the fillets in a single layer. Place them on the sauce and pour over the remainder.
5 Bake for about 25 minutes, then let cool to room temperature before serving.
KCal 391 P 26g C 4g S 277mg SFA 3g UFA 25g

FISH CURRY

This recipe is from Sri Lanka, but similar versions are found around the coast of southern India and along the Malay peninsula. If you cannot get tamarind paste, use a little lime or lemon juice instead.

INGREDIENTS

2 tbsp mustard or coconut oil
½ tsp fenugreek seeds, lightly crushed
2 onions, sliced
2 garlic cloves, sliced
1 tbsp chopped fresh ginger
½ tsp turmeric
1½ tsp ground cinnamon
1½ tsp ground coriander
2 tsp cumin, dry-roasted and ground
3–5 green chilies, seeded and sliced
1 stalk lemongrass, bottom part only, finely sliced
2 pieces pandanus leaf, 2in (5cm) long
2 sprays curry leaves
1 tbsp tamarind paste
2½ cups (600ml) thick coconut milk
salt, optional
1½lb (750g) butterfish, red snapper, sea bass, or other firm white fish steaks

PREPARATION

1 Heat the oil in a large heavy pan and quickly sauté the fenugreek seeds until they start to darken. Add the onions and cook gently until they turn a light gold, 5–10 minutes. Then add the garlic and ginger and cook, stirring frequently, for another 2–3 minutes. Do not let them brown.
2 Stir in the spices and herbs – the turmeric, cinnamon, coriander, cumin, chilies, lemongrass, pandanus, and curry leaves.
3 Stir the tamarind paste into a few tablespoons of water in a bowl and let blend for several minutes, then strain into the pan.
4 Pour in half the coconut milk. (Put canned coconut milk in the freezer for an hour or two first, so that the thick milk collects at the top. You will need two cans to get sufficient thick milk. The sauce will be too thin if you try to make do with one. If using creamed coconut, make a thick milk by combining 1 cup (250g) with 1⅔ cups (400ml) water.) Simmer for 10 minutes, then taste and salt lightly if necessary.
5 Put in the pieces of fish and the rest of the coconut milk. Bring to a boil, then reduce the heat and let the curry simmer for 5–10 minutes, depending on the thickness of the fish. Serve with plain rice garnished with a little fresh cilantro.
KCal 660 P 33g C 12g S 167mg SFA 45g UFA 6g

Coriander

Turmeric

Ginger

Garlic

Onions

Fenugreek

Mustard oil

Butterfish

Green
chilies

Cumin

Cinnamon

Lemongrass

Pandanus

Curry
leaves

Tamarind
paste

Coconut
milk

Salt

GRILLED BABY OCTOPUS

These days baby octopus can be bought at supermarket fish counters and enterprising fishmongers. Large octopus can be grilled, too, but first put the cleaned octopus in a large pan of water with a couple of bay leaves and some parsley stalks and simmer for 1–1½ hours, until nearly tender. Drain, cut the octopus into bite-sized pieces when cool, and then marinate. Serves 4–6.

INGREDIENTS

large bunch of basil
large bunch of cilantro
juice of 2 limes
3 tbsp white vinegar
4 tbsp sunflower oil
2 tbsp mango chutney
salt
red pepper flakes, to taste
2lb (1kg) baby octopus, cleaned

PREPARATION

1 Remove and discard the thick stems from the basil and cilantro, then coarsely chop the herbs and mix together with all the other ingredients except the octopus.
2 Put the octopus in a large bowl and pour the herb mixture over. Let marinate in the refrigerator for several hours.
3 Lift out the octopus and barbecue or broil it for about a minute on each side. You may find it easier to thread the octopus on skewers. If you use the wooden kind, soak them in water for a few minutes first so that they do not burn easily. Heat the marinade through and serve it as a sauce, if you wish. Some bread and a mixed herb salad make good accompaniments.
KCal 385 P47g C 7g S 203mg SFA 3g UFA 14g

VARIATION

Small squid can be grilled in the same way, but the cooking time will probably need to be a little longer, 2–3 minutes per side, depending on the size of the squid. Allow 3–5 squid per person, according to whether you are serving the dish as a first or as a main course.

EEL IN GREEN SAUCE

Eel in green sauce is a popular dish throughout Belgium and Holland, but it is made in a slightly different way in the two countries. In Holland, cream and egg yolks are not used and the herbs may be lightly cooked in water before being added to the eel. The Belgian version given here is a richer, more rewarding dish, although the flavors of the herbs are less pronounced than in the more austere Dutch version. It can be eaten hot or cold.

INGREDIENTS

3lb (1.5kg) small eels, gutted
6 tbsp (90g) butter
2 shallots, finely chopped
¾lb (400g) young spinach, shredded
1lb (500g) sorrel, shredded
large handful of chervil, chopped
large handful of flat-leaf parsley, chopped
a few nettle leaves, chopped (optional)
leaves from 2 sprigs sage, chopped
leaves from 2 sprigs summer or winter savory, chopped
leaves from 2 sprigs thyme, chopped
leaves from 2 sprigs tarragon, chopped
¾ cup (180ml) dry white wine
salt and black pepper
¼ cup (60ml) heavy cream
2 egg yolks, beaten
juice of ½ lemon

PREPARATION

1 Ask the fishmonger to skin the eel, or with a sharp small knife loosen the skin around the top of the body. Grasp firmly and pull downward toward the tail. Paper towels will give a better grip. This task is very easy to do but takes confidence.
2 Cut the eels into 2in (5cm) segments, discarding the heads.
3 Heat the butter in a wide pan and gently soften the shallots. Add the eel, sauté for a couple of minutes, then stir in the spinach and herbs. Cover and sweat for 5 minutes.
4 Pour over the wine, season with salt and pepper, and cook over low heat until tender, about 10 minutes. If necessary, add more wine or water.
5 Whisk together the cream, egg yolks, and some of the lemon juice. Taste; you may need more, depending on the sharpness of the sorrel.
6 Remove the eel using a slotted spoon, and keep warm if you are going to serve it hot. Take the pan from the heat and stir in the cream and egg mixture. Heat through very gently for a minute – it must not boil – then pour the sauce over the eel. Serve accompanied by new potatoes or bread.
KCal 851 P 61g C 10g S 790mg SFA 24g UFA 30g

STUFFED TURBOT

This is an elegant dish with a fine flavor. The same stuffing can be used with sole, but you would need to allow one fish per person. Serves 2.

INGREDIENTS

1 turbot, weighing 1½–2lb (750g–1kg)
2 tbsp dried bread crumbs
1–2 tbsp olive oil
Stuffing
2 bacon slices, finely chopped
2 mushrooms, finely chopped
2 scallions, or 3 Welsh onions, tops only, chopped
3–4 Chinese or ordinary chives, chopped
2 tbsp chopped flat-leaf parsley
1 tbsp chopped thyme leaves
1 tbsp chopped summer savory leaves
2 tbsp fresh bread crumbs
1 egg, lightly beaten
Sauce
2 shallots, finely chopped
½ cup (125ml) dry white wine
1 tbsp chopped flat-leaf parsley
2 tbsp chopped basil
1 tbsp chopped summer savory leaves
2 tbsp chopped salad burnet
salt and black pepper
scant ½ cup (100ml) sour cream

PREPARATION

1 Keep the turbot whole, but remove the upper dark skin by cutting it across where the tail joins the body. Loosen the skin with the tip of the knife until you can grasp it firmly, then hold the tail down with one hand and pull the skin toward the head with the other.
2 Cut along the backbone with a sharp knife, then lift the flesh of the fillets on either side, cutting out toward the sides. Fold them back and remove the backbone. To do this, bend the fish until the backbone breaks in the middle. Repeat the procedure so that it breaks in 3–4 places, then take out the bones.
3 Heat the oven to 350°F/180°C.
4 Prepare the stuffing by frying the bacon in its own fat, adding a little olive oil if necessary. Add the mushrooms and cook until softened, then put in the scallions and herbs. Mix in enough bread crumbs to give a medium-firm consistency and bind with most of the egg.
5 Put the turbot into a lightly oiled baking dish, and fill the cavity with the stuffing.
6 Draw up the fillets over the stuffing and brush the top of the fish with the remaining beaten egg.

Cover with a light coating of dried bread crumbs, drizzle olive oil over the top, and bake in the oven for about 25 minutes. Shape any leftover stuffing into little patties and fry as an accompaniment.
7 To prepare the sauce, cook the shallots in the wine until the liquid has reduced by two-thirds, then add the herbs and season with salt and pepper. Stir in the sour cream, let it just heat through, and serve with the fish.
KCal 700 P 49g C 24g S 949mg SFA 14g UFA 22g

HAKE IN SALSA VERDE

This salsa verde of parsley and garlic comes from the Basque country. The dish is customarily prepared with hake (a much underrated fish outside the Iberian peninsula), but another firm white fish such as haddock or cod could be used. Choose thick fillets cut from a large fish. It is best made in an earthenware casserole that can be put on the top of the stove on a heat diffuser.

INGREDIENTS

1½lb (750g) hake fillets
salt
6 tbsp olive oil
3 garlic cloves, chopped
5 tbsp chopped parsley

PREPARATION

1 Sprinkle the fillets with a little salt. Heat the oil in the casserole over medium heat and add the garlic. Let it color gently, taking care that the oil does not get too hot.
2 Add the hake fillets, laying them side by side, scatter with parsley, and cover the casserole. Shake frequently as they cook.
3 After 5 minutes remove the lid – the hake will have released some liquid into the dish. Turn the heat to low and continue to cook, uncovered, shaking the dish gently and, if necessary, spooning some of the cooking liquid over the fillets.
4 Cook for 5–7 minutes longer, depending on the thickness of the fish. The sauce should emulsify and thicken during the last minutes of cooking. Serve from the casserole.
KCal 382 P 34g C 1g S 291mg SFA 4g UFA 21g

MEAT DISHES

Stews, casseroles, and braised meats are inconceivable without herbs; a few sprigs of a single herb, or a bouquet garni, will add depth of flavor to all slow-cooked dishes. Put herbs into marinades and sauces, or throw stalks on the barbecue to add aroma to grills.

PORK FAJITAS IN CHILI SAUCE WITH SALSA FRESCA

The fajitas have typical Mexican flavorings of chili and dried herbs – use Mexican or Mediterranean oregano. The moderately pungent dried pasilla chilies could be replaced by other dried varieties – anchos, mulatos, or smoky chipotles. In Mexican and Southwest cooking, dried chilies are toasted and rehydrated before use.

INGREDIENTS

3 pasilla chilies
3lb (1.5kg) boneless pork loin
½ tsp ground cumin
3 tsp dried oregano
3 tsp dried thyme
juice of 1 lime
juice of ½ orange
½ small onion, sliced
2 garlic cloves
4 tbsp olive oil
Salsa Fresca
4 large ripe tomatoes, peeled, seeded, and chopped
1 red onion, finely chopped
4 pickled or fresh jalapeño chilies
6 tbsp coarsely chopped cilantro leaves
juice of 1 lime
2 tbsp tequila
salt

PREPARATION

1 Heat the oven to 475°F/240°C. Remove the stems from the chilies and shake out the seeds. Toast them in the oven for 2–3 minutes. Do not let them burn. Transfer them to a bowl, cover with boiling water, and soak for 30 minutes.
2 Remove any fat or connective tissue from the meat, then cut it into chunks about 3in (7cm) long. Cut the chunks into flat strips about ¾in (2cm) wide and put them in a glass or china bowl.
3 Purée together the rest of the ingredients (except those for the salsa). Add the chilies and blend with enough of their soaking liquid to make a marinade that will cover the pork. Pour this over the meat, cover with plastic wrap and refrigerate for 3–4 hours, or longer if you wish.
4 Make the salsa fresca by combining all the ingredients. Cover and refrigerate for at least 30 minutes before serving.
5 Prepare the barbecue or preheat the broiler. Take the pork out of the marinade, reserving the latter. Thread the meat on skewers, weaving the skewers in and out along the strips. I find wooden ones the best; if you are going to put them on the barbecue, soak them in water for a few minutes first. Grill over the fire or on a lightly greased tray under a broiler for 8–10 minutes, turning once.
6 Heat the marinade to serve as a sauce and accompany with salsa fresca and tortillas or rice.
KCal 721 P 75g C 10g S 381mg SFA 11g UFA 26g

CHICKEN BREASTS WITH LEMON BALM SALSA

This easily prepared dish is good eaten hot or cold.

INGREDIENTS

4 boneless, skinned chicken breasts
3 tbsp lemon juice
4 tbsp olive oil
coarsely ground black pepper
4 tbsp chopped lemon balm leaves
lemon balm sprigs, to garnish
Lemon Balm Salsa
2 tbsp sunflower seeds
1 medium red onion, coarsely chopped
8 sun-dried tomatoes, chopped
3 tbsp chopped lemon balm leaves
salt and black pepper
juice of ½ lemon
1 tbsp lemon balm vinegar (see page 136)
6–8 tbsp (90–120ml) olive oil

PREPARATION

1 Marinate the chicken breasts in the lemon juice, olive oil, black pepper, and lemon balm for a few hours in the refrigerator, turning the pieces once.
2 Toss the sunflower seeds in a hot skillet without oil, dry-roasting them until slightly browned. Grind them coarsely. Mix with all the other ingredients for the salsa. Put it in the refrigerator and allow at least 30 minutes for the flavors to blend before serving.
3 Lift out the meat from the marinade and broil it for about 10 minutes, turning once. Heat the marinade separately in a pan.
4 Arrange the chicken pieces on a serving dish, strain over the cooking liquids, and garnish with lemon balm. Serve the salsa separately.
KCal 649 P 31g C 7g S 396mg SFA 8g UFA 45g

VARIATIONS

Lemon balm salsa makes an excellent partner for other grilled meat and fish dishes.

VIETNAMESE CHICKEN AND EGGPLANT PUREE

This recipe is a version of a dish found in Vietnam and Laos, where it is sometimes made with fish or shellfish instead of chicken. The use of lots of herbs and the way of rolling the purée in lettuce leaves is particularly Vietnamese. Serves 6.

INGREDIENTS

1 lb (500g) boneless, skinned chicken breasts or thighs
6 small round Asian eggplants (white, green, or purple)
4 tbsp chopped Chinese chives
3 fresh chilies, seeded and sliced
3 tbsp chopped mint

Dipping Sauce
2 tbsp fish sauce
3 tbsp rice vinegar
1–2 finely sliced chilies
a few shredded mint leaves
pinch or more of sugar, to taste

To Serve
leaves from 1–2 firm-leaf lettuces, such as romaine
handful of mint leaves
handful of rao ram or cilantro leaves
handful of sweet basil leaves
handful of fine dill sprigs
a few Chinese chives, cut into short lengths

PREPARATION

1 Put the chicken pieces in a pan with enough cold water just to cover and bring to a boil. Lower the heat and simmer for 8–10 minutes, depending on their size. Strain, reserving the liquid. Shred the meat when cool.

2 Heat the oven to 400°F/200°C. Prick the eggplants in 2–3 places with a fork and bake for about 10 minutes, until soft. Let cool, then remove the skins.

3 Combine the ingredients for the dipping sauce and put into small dishes or saucers to serve.

4 Blend the cooked chicken, eggplants, Chinese chives, chilies, mint, and 1–2 tablespoons of the poaching liquid in a food processor or pound them to a purée. This should be quite thick, but add a little more liquid if necessary.

5 To serve in the Vietnamese style, arrange the lettuce and herb leaves on platters and put the purée in a bowl. Everyone takes a lettuce leaf, places on it some herb leaves and a spoonful of purée, rolls it up, and dips it in the sauce.

KCal 162 P 23g C 9g S 286mg SFA 1g UFA 2g

PAUPIETTES OF VEAL

Called blinde vinken *in Holland, and* Rouladen *in Germany, these small stuffed rolls of veal are popular in many Western countries. They can also be made with beef, but then the cooking time must be extended. Serves 6.*

INGREDIENTS

2–3 tbsp sunflower oil
2 shallots, finely chopped
4 garlic cloves, finely chopped
¼lb (125g) bacon, chopped
2 thick slices stale firm bread, crusts removed
6 tbsp chopped flat-leaf parsley
2 tsp chopped lemon thyme leaves
2 tsp chopped micromeria or savory leaves
2 tbsp pine nuts, optional
black pepper
grinding of nutmeg
1 egg
6 veal scaloppine, beaten very thin and trimmed (see opposite)
½ cup dry white wine
scant 1 cup (200ml) veal or chicken stock, or water

PREPARATION

1 Heat 1 tablespoon of the oil in a skillet and gently cook the shallots, garlic, and bacon until all are turning golden.

2 Put the bread through a blender to make coarse crumbs. Pour them into a bowl and add the shallots, garlic, and bacon from the pan together with the herbs, pine nuts, and meat trimmings. Season well with pepper and nutmeg and stir in the egg to bind the mixture.

3 Spread out the pieces of veal and season lightly if you wish. Put a spoonful of the stuffing at one end of each, then roll up and secure with toothpicks or string (see opposite).

4 Heat the oven to 325°F/160°C.

5 Heat the remaining oil in a pan that will take the paupiettes in one layer and can also go in the oven. Brown them lightly on all sides, then add the wine and simmer for a few minutes more, turning once or twice. Add the stock and bring to a boil.

6 Cover the pan with a lid or foil and transfer to the oven. Cook for 45–50 minutes, until the meat is tender.

7 Remove the paupiettes to a warm serving platter and boil down the cooking juices to make a sauce. A purée of fava beans flavored with savory or mint, or some mashed potatoes, makes a good accompaniment.

KCal 378 P 35g C 9g S 604mg SFA 6g UFA 14g

PREPARING THE PAUPIETTES

  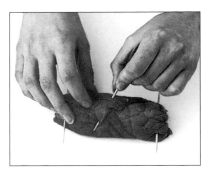

1 *Lay the scaloppine between two sheets of plastic wrap or waxed paper and lightly pound with a mallet or rolling pin until about ⅛in (3mm) thick. Trim the edges to a neat shape.*

2 *Put a spoonful of herb stuffing at the end of each piece of veal. Roll it up, not too tightly as the filling will expand a little during cooking, but not so loosely that the stuffing falls out.*

3 *Secure the rolls with toothpicks, turning in the ends if the pieces of meat are large enough. Alternatively, you can tie them around once or twice with a piece of fine string.*

IRANIAN LAMB AND HERB STEW

A richly flavored stew of beans, lamb, herbs, and dried limes. The limes are a specialty of Iran and can be found in Iranian shops, as can powdered dried lime. However, it is easy to dry limes yourself if you leave them on a radiator for several months until they are hard and sound hollow when tapped. Fenugreek is an essential herb for this stew. It is easy to grow in summer, but it can also be bought dried from Iranian and Indian shops.

INGREDIENTS

½ cup (100g) red kidney beans, soaked overnight
4 tbsp sunflower oil
1 large onion, chopped
1lb (500g) lean lamb, cubed
1 tsp turmeric
black pepper and salt
juice of 2 lemons
2–3 leeks, finely chopped
½lb (250g) spinach, chopped
about 7 cups (200g) flat-leaf parsley, chopped
about 2 cups (60g) cilantro or celery leaves, chopped
leaves from a few sprigs fresh fenugreek
or 1 tbsp dried leaves
5 dried limes

PREPARATION

1 Strain the beans and cook in fresh unsalted water for 15–20 minutes, then drain them, rinse, and set aside.
2 Heat half the oil in a large heavy pan and sauté the onion. Add the lamb and brown it on all sides. Stir in the turmeric and season with pepper and a little salt. Pour over the lemon juice and just enough boiling water to cover the meat. Cover and simmer for 30 minutes.
3 Heat the remaining oil and sauté the leeks, spinach, and herbs for 10–15 minutes, until they darken. Add this mixture to the meat along with the beans.
4 Pierce the limes in 2–3 places and add them to the pan. Make sure there is enough liquid just to cover all the ingredients and simmer for an hour, checking occasionally that nothing is sticking.
5 Serve with rice. Although they are not eaten, the limes are usually left in the dish.
KCal 478 P 38g C 20g S 326mg SFA 7g UFA 18g

VARIATION

Black-eyed peas can be used as an alternative to red kidney beans.

GUINEA FOWL WITH YOUNG GARLIC AND HERBS

Fresh garlic is in the stores in late spring. The dish can be made at other times of the year with dried garlic. As with fresh, separate the cloves and remove the outer papery layers, but do not peel them. The delicate flavor of new garlic is particularly suited to guinea fowl; with older garlic, a chicken might be a better choice. Illustrated on page 98.

INGREDIENTS

⅓ cup (90ml) olive oil
1 guinea fowl, weighing approximately 3lb (1.5kg)
2 heads fresh garlic
2 long sprigs rosemary
6–8 sprigs thyme
2 bay leaves
4 sprigs sage
6–8 sprigs parsley
2 sprigs costmary, optional
juice of 1 lemon
salt and black pepper
chopped parsley, to garnish

PREPARATION

1 Heat the oven to 350°F/180°C.
2 Pour a tablespoon of the oil into a skillet and brown the guinea fowl lightly on all sides.
3 Split the heads of garlic into cloves. There is no need to peel fresh new garlic, but it is better to snip off the long tapering skins at the tops of the cloves. Pour the rest of the oil into a deep casserole dish, just large enough to hold the bird, and add the garlic.
4 Tie the herbs into three small mixed bundles. (This makes it easier to remove them later.) Put one inside the guinea fowl, then put the bird on top of the garlic with the other two herb bouquets on either side. Pour over the lemon juice and season with salt and pepper.
5 Cover the dish with a double layer of foil as well as the lid, to seal it as tight as possible, and cook for 1½ hours.
6 Lift out the guinea fowl and let rest for 10 minutes in a warm place. Discard the herbs and strain the garlic, reserving the pan juices. Pass the garlic through a sieve or mash it with a fork.
7 Pour off as much excess oil as possible, then reheat the pan juices and pour them into a sauce boat to serve. Carve the guinea fowl and arrange on a serving platter. Add the garlic purée and garnish with a little parsley.
KCal 440 P 32g C 7g S 142mg SFA 6g UFA 23g

JAMBON PERSILLE

This is the traditional Easter dish of Burgundy, marbled pink and green and set in a pale gold aspic. The local charcutiers make it with a whole ham, but it can be made at home using a ham steak. Illustrated on page 98. Serves 8–10.

INGREDIENTS

4lb (2kg) ham steak
2 carrots, chopped
4 garlic cloves, chopped
2 calf's feet
large bouquet garni made up of bay leaves and sprigs of thyme, tarragon, and flat-leaf parsley
2 onions, each stuck with 1 clove
8 black peppercorns
1 bottle dry white wine
3 shallots
about 2 cups (60g) flat-leaf parsley
3–4 tbsp white wine vinegar

PREPARATION

1 Soak the ham for 18–24 hours to remove excess salt, changing the water two or three times. Drain and set aside.
2 Put the carrots and garlic in a large pan with the calf's feet, bouquet garni, onions, and peppercorns. Place the ham in the middle, pour over the wine, and enough water to cover.
3 Bring to a boil, skim, and lower the heat. Simmer gently for 3–4 hours, adding more water if necessary. Skim the surface when needed, to remove fat. When the ham pierces easily with a fork, remove the pan from the heat and let cool slightly. Lift out the ham. Discard the calf's feet.
4 Boil down the stock to about 4 cups (1 liter) and skim thoroughly. Strain through a sieve lined with a double layer of cheesecloth. Taste and add pepper if necessary – it should be quite highly seasoned.
5 Chop the shallots and parsley and mix together.
6 Pull the ham into large chunks with your fingers or using two forks. Put a layer in the bottom of a large glass or china bowl, then a layer of parsley. Sprinkle over a spoonful of vinegar and ladleful of stock, letting them run down between the pieces of ham. Repeat the layers until the ham and parsley are used up, then pour over the remaining stock.
7 Press down the meat, making sure all is below the liquid. Cover with a plate of almost the same diameter as the bowl, put a weight on top, and chill for 12 hours. Serve from the bowl, or unmold, as you wish. Small gherkins are a good accompaniment, and some crusty bread.

KCal 671 P 45g C 4g S 2967mg SFA 18g UFA 26g

PORK AND CRAB SALAD

A fresh-tasting salad in which the ingredients can be varied according to what is available: chicken and shrimp may replace the pork and crab, white or red radish may be added. The inspiration for the salad is Vietnamese, so bean sprouts and bamboo shoots in place of the tomato and pepper would make it quite authentic. It is important to have a variety of herbs, but they can be changed to suit your taste. Try lemon or sweet basil, cilantro in place of rao ram, anise or anise hyssop for the fennel, catnip or calamint for the mint. Serve as a first course. Illustrated on page 99.

INGREDIENTS

¼lb (100g) piece of pork loin
¼lb (100g) white crabmeat, cooked
1 tbsp sesame seeds
lettuce leaves
2 plum tomatoes, seeded and sliced into strips
2 green peppers, preferably the long, pale green type, seeded and sliced into strips
½ cucumber, very thinly sliced
3 scallions, finely sliced
2 carrots, cut into slivers
4 sprigs Thai basil
3–4 sprigs fennel
6 sprigs rao ram
4 sprigs mint
Nuoc Cham Dressing
2 tbsp unsalted peanuts
1 tbsp chili oil
2 tsp sugar, or to taste
4 tbsp water
4 tbsp fish sauce
5–6 tbsp (75–90ml) lime juice

PREPARATION

1 Put the pork in a pan with just enough cold water to cover. Bring to a boil, reduce the heat, and simmer until tender, about 20 minutes. Leave in the water for 10 minutes. Strain and let cool.
2 Shred the crabmeat and slice the pork into very thin rounds. Dry-roast the sesame seeds until golden (for method, see page 93).
3 Line a platter with lettuce leaves. Arrange the tomatoes, peppers, cucumber, scallions, carrots, and herb leaves on the lettuce. Top with the pork and crabmeat. Scatter the sesame seeds on top.
4 To make the nuoc cham dressing, dry-roast the peanuts until they have darkened a little. Coarsely grind them and mix with all the other dressing ingredients. Stir well, then spoon it over and serve.

KCal 233 P 16g C 18g S 766mg SFA 2g UFA 9g

Jambon Persillé
(see previous page)

Guinea Fowl with
Young Garlic and Herbs
(see page 96)

*Pork and Crab Salad
(see page 97)*

ARISTA ALLA FIORENTINA
Italian roast pork with rosemary

Illustrated on page 65. Serves 6.

INGREDIENTS

*2lb (1kg) pork loin, boned and with the skin and
most of the fat removed
a few sprigs rosemary
2 garlic cloves, finely chopped
salt and black pepper
a few crushed cloves or juniper berries, optional
2 tbsp olive oil
½ cup dry white wine or water*

PREPARATION

1 Heat the oven to 350°F/180°C.
2 Cut a deep slit lengthwise down the pork, making sure it does not pierce the other side.
3 Strip the rosemary leaves from the stems, chop them fine, and mix with the garlic. Put some of the mixture into the pocket in the meat and spread the rest over the flesh. Season.
4 Roll up the meat and tie around with string at regular intervals. Rub the outside of the roll with the crushed cloves and put into a roasting pan that has been lightly greased with 1 tablespoon of the oil. Pour the remaining oil over the pork.
5 Put the roast in the oven and allow it to brown, turning once or twice. Pour over the wine and continue to cook for an hour or so, basting occasionally, until most of the liquid has evaporated and the meat is cooked through.
6 Let the roast rest for 10 minutes before thinly slicing it. Arista is good eaten hot or cold.
KCal 305 P 35g C 1g S 128mg SFA 5g UFA 10g

LAMB KLEFTIKO
Baked lamb with oregano

This Greek village dish uses thick slices cut from a leg of lamb across the bone, but it also works well with large chops. In Greece it would be made with rigani (dried oregano, see pages 16–17). Baking parchment for wrapping the bundles will look more attractive than foil. Illustrated on page 65.

INGREDIENTS

*4 slices cut from a leg of lamb, about 1½in (4cm) thick
5 tbsp (75ml) olive oil
1 large garlic clove, cut into slivers
salt and black pepper
2 tbsp chopped fresh oregano, or 1 tbsp dried
juice of 1 lemon*

PREPARATION

1 Heat the oven to 400°F/200°C.
2 Cut 4 pieces of baking parchment or foil, large enough to wrap the pieces of lamb individually, and brush with a tablespoon of oil.
3 Wipe the meat, taking care to remove any splinters of bone, and place each slice in the center of a piece of parchment or foil. Make some small incisions and stud the meat with slivers of garlic. Season and scatter over the oregano. Sprinkle with lemon juice and the remaining oil.
4 Close the bundles neatly, folding and crimping the edges or tying them to make sure they cannot leak. Bake in the oven for 10 minutes, then reduce the heat to 350°F/180°C and continue to cook for 40 minutes longer.
5 Undo the bundles but serve in the wrapping.
KCal 455 P 29g C 1g S 87mg SFA 12g UFA 23g

SALTIMBOCCA ALLA ROMANA
Veal with prosciutto and sage

A quickly cooked dish to serve with puréed or sautéed potatoes or a celeriac purée flavored with lovage. Pound the scaloppine as shown on page 95. The dish is illustrated on page 64.

INGREDIENTS

*4 large thin slices of prosciutto
8 veal scaloppine, about 5in (12cm) square
8 sage leaves
4 tbsp butter
salt and black pepper
¼ cup (75ml) dry white wine*

PREPARATION

1 Cut the slices of prosciutto in half. Put one piece on top of each scaloppine, trimming it if necessary, then top each with a sage leaf, pinning the layers together with toothpicks.
2 Heat the butter in a skillet large enough to hold the scaloppine in a single layer. Put in the meat, veal side down, and cook for 2–3 minutes, then turn and cook the other side. Season.
3 Pour over the wine. When it bubbles, lift out the meat, remove the toothpicks, leaving the sage leaves on top, and keep warm. Scrape any bits from the bottom of the pan, pour the juices over the meat, and serve. The whole process should not take more than about 5 minutes.
KCal 296 P 33g C neg S 574mg SFA 10g UFA 6g

GRILLED STEAK WITH BEARNAISE SAUCE

Illustrated on page 64.

INGREDIENTS

4 fillet or sirloin steaks
olive oil
salt and black pepper
Béarnaise Sauce
⅔ cup (150ml) dry white wine
3 tbsp white wine or tarragon vinegar
3 shallots, finely chopped
5 sprigs tarragon
freshly ground white pepper
¼lb plus 4 tbsp (175g) unsalted butter
3 egg yolks
salt
1 tbsp finely chopped tarragon leaves or a mixture of tarragon and chervil

PREPARATION

1 To make the sauce, put the white wine, vinegar, shallots, sprigs of tarragon, and a good grinding of white pepper in a small heavy pan over low heat. Simmer, uncovered, for 10–15 minutes, until the liquid has reduced to 2–3 tablespoons.
2 Strain through a fine sieve, pressing the shallots and tarragon well to extract all the flavor. Return the liquid to the pan.
3 Melt the butter over low heat in a separate small pan and set aside. When it has cooled to lukewarm, pour off the clear liquid to use later and discard the white residue.
4 Set the pan with the wine and vinegar infusion over very low heat and whisk in the egg yolks and a little salt. Then add the melted butter, a tablespoon or so at a time, whisking continuously. Do not add more butter until each spoonful has been absorbed. Remove the pan from the heat before adding the final spoonful – it will still be hot enough to continue cooking the sauce.
5 Stir in the finely chopped tarragon and check the seasoning.
6 Prepare the barbecue or preheat the broiler. Rub the steaks lightly on both sides with olive oil and season with salt and pepper just before putting them on the broiler.
7 Sear the meat on both sides, about 1 minute per side. The rest of the broiling time will depend on the thickness of the steaks and how well you like them cooked. For a 2–2½in (5–6cm) thick fillet steak, allow a total cooking time, including searing, of 6–8 minutes for rare; 8–10 minutes for medium rare; 10–12 minutes for medium. For a 1in (2½–3cm) thick sirloin steak allow 5–6 minutes for rare; 6–7 for medium rare; and 7–9 for medium. It is best not to turn the meat more than once while broiling in order to preserve the juices that collect on the top. Serve with the sauce.
KCal 723 P 40g C 3g S 186mg SFA 32g UFA 22g

VARIATION

By substituting mint for tarragon in the béarnaise sauce you can make *sauce paloise*. Fine and sharply flavored, this makes an excellent accompaniment for broiled chicken and meat or poached salmon.

PORK NOISETTES WITH FENNEL

Illustrated on pages 64–65.

INGREDIENTS

3–4 tbsp olive oil
10 shallots, finely chopped
2 tsp crushed fennel seeds
salt and black pepper
8 pork noisettes
bunch of fennel
2 bay leaves
½ cup (125ml) Calvados

PREPARATION

1 Lightly oil an ovenproof dish large enough to hold the noisettes in a single layer. Make a bed of shallots and fennel seeds in the bottom, season lightly with salt and pepper, and put the meat on top. Season again.
2 Cut most of the fennel leaves from the stems. Reserve the leaves, but strew the stems and bay leaves around and over the meat. Dribble a little olive oil over the surface. If you can, prepare the dish to this point a few hours before you want to cook it so that the meat has time to start absorbing the flavors of the herbs.
3 Heat the broiler. Set the oven to 300°F/150°C.
4 Put the dish under the broiler for 2–4 minutes, depending on the thickness of the noisettes, so that they color slightly. Pour over the Calvados, cover tightly with foil, and put the dish in the oven to cook slowly for 45–50 minutes. Check after 20 minutes and turn the noisettes.
5 Finely chop the fennel leaves. Before serving, remove the fennel stems and bay leaves. Scatter the fennel leaves over the meat and serve straight from the dish. The noisettes are excellent eaten with mashed sweet potatoes, flavored with a little sherry and chopped parsley, and a green salad.
KCal 484 P 43g C 11g S 160mg SFA 7g UFA 17g

101

VEGETABLE DISHES

Herbs are usually added to vegetables as a last-minute garnish, but they can play a more substantial role. Provençal vegetable dishes are always aromatic with herbs; the Turks excel in flavoring vegetable dishes with combinations of dill, mint, and parsley.

TIAN OF TOMATOES AND PEPPERS

A tian is a shallow earthenware dish from Provence that has given its name to the vegetable dishes cooked in it. Serves 6.

INGREDIENTS

4 red peppers
6 large tomatoes
10 anchovy fillets
large handful of basil leaves
1 tbsp chopped thyme leaves
½ tbsp chopped winter savory leaves
3 garlic cloves, chopped
½ cup (75g) small black olives
black pepper
4–5 tbsp freshly made bread crumbs
3–4 tbsp olive oil

PREPARATION

1 Broil the peppers or put them on a gas flame. Turn frequently until charred on all sides. Cool in a heavy plastic bag, then skin them under cold running water. Halve the peppers and remove ribs and seeds. Dry on paper towels and cut into slices.
2 Heat the oven to 400°F/200°C.
3 Immerse the tomatoes in boiling water for a few seconds. Drain and peel them and cut into thick slices. Cut the anchovy fillets in half and tear the basil leaves into small pieces.
4 Lightly oil a tian or other gratin dish and line the bottom with a layer of tomatoes (about a third). Spread over them half the anchovies, a sprinkling of herbs and garlic, and half the olives. Season with black pepper. Cover with a layer of half the peppers, followed by another layer of tomatoes. Repeat the anchovies, herbs, garlic, olives, and black pepper seasoning. Add the rest of the peppers and a final layer of tomatoes.
5 Scatter the bread crumbs on top, drizzle over the oil, and bake for 30 minutes. Serve warm or cold, but not chilled.
KCal 188 P 5g C 16g S 673mg SFA 2g UFA 8g

Winter savory

Thyme

Basil

Anchovy fillets

Red peppers   *Tomatoes*

Garlic

Black olives

Black
pepper

Fresh
bread crumbs

Olive oil

FAVA BEANS IN OLIVE OIL

In this Turkish-inspired dish, the water evaporates during the slow cooking, leaving a rich sauce that is not at all greasy. Shelled older beans can be used, but you will need to increase the quantity.

INGREDIENTS

2lb (1kg) fresh young fava beans, in their pods
salt
juice of ½ lemon
2 bunches of scallions, cut into short lengths
4 tbsp chopped summer savory
6 tbsp chopped dill or anise hyssop
2 tsp sugar
½ cup (100ml) olive oil
scant 1 cup (200ml) water
yogurt and garlic, to serve (optional)

PREPARATION

1 Trim the bean pods, cutting the larger ones in half (young beans do not need shelling). Sprinkle them with salt and pour over the lemon juice.
2 Put about a third of the beans, including all the larger pods, in the bottom of a heavy pan and spread half the scallions and half the herbs over them. Add another layer of beans, the rest of the scallions and herbs, and then top with the last of the beans.
3 Sprinkle over the sugar, and add the olive oil and water. Cover the pan with a sheet of moistened waxed paper and a tight-fitting lid. Cook over moderate heat for about an hour, shaking the pan occasionally to prevent sticking. The beans should be tender but still whole.
4 Remove from the heat and let cool in the pan. Put the beans in a serving dish and serve cool or cold. If you wish, accompany them with a bowl of yogurt flavored with crushed garlic.
KCal 387 P 15g C 21g S 109mg SFA 4g UFA 22g

JERUSALEM ARTICHOKES WITH PIEDS DE MOUTON

Pieds de mouton mushrooms have a particular affinity for Jerusalem artichokes, just as chanterelles have for Chinese artichokes (crosnes). Here are two recipes in one, the difference being in the preparation of the artichokes.

INGREDIENTS

1lb (500g) Jerusalem artichokes
juice of ½ lemon
4 tbsp butter
1lb (500g) pieds de mouton
3 shallots, finely chopped
1 tbsp chopped thyme
1 tbsp chopped marjoram
2 tbsp chopped flat-leaf parsley
salt and black pepper
½ cup dry white wine or sherry
2–3 tbsp heavy cream, optional

PREPARATION

1 Peel the artichokes, cut into pieces, and drop into water and lemon juice. Blanch them for 2–3 minutes in fresh boiling water and drain. Melt half the butter and sauté them until almost tender.
2 Wipe the mushrooms and cut into similar pieces. Heat the rest of the butter and sauté the shallots until soft, turn up the heat, and add the mushrooms. Sauté briskly for 2–3 minutes, then add the artichokes and herbs and season well. Pour over the wine, cover, and simmer for 5 minutes.
3 Put the vegetables in a serving dish. Boil down the liquid, if necessary, and stir in a little cream.
KCal 201 P 5g C 14g S 127mg SFA 8g UFA 4g

VARIATION

For an even more delicate dish, trim Chinese artichokes. Simmer for 5 minutes in enough water to cover plus a little butter. Drain, reserving the liquid. Cook the shallots and chanterelles as above; add the herbs and artichokes with a little cooking liquid instead of wine. Simmer for 3–4 minutes.

STUFFED CABBAGE WITH HYSSOP

A hearty dish to serve as a main course with good bread or potatoes. Serves 6.

INGREDIENTS

1 large green cabbage
¾ cup (100g) rice
2 tbsp olive oil
1 large onion, finely chopped
3 garlic cloves, finely chopped
¼lb (150g) piece of bacon or spek (a north European specialty bacon), cubed
2 large tomatoes, peeled, seeded, and chopped
1 cup (100g) shelled peas
½lb (250g) sausage meat or minced pork
2 tbsp chopped hyssop leaves
salt and black pepper
approximately 3 cups (750ml) chicken or vegetable stock
sprigs of hyssop, to garnish

PREPARATION

1 Trim away the outermost leaves from the cabbage and cut off the stalk. Blanch the cabbage for 5 minutes in boiling water. Refresh it with cold water and drain well. Carefully separate the leaves. Cut out the lower part of the central rib of the biggest leaves.
2 Parboil the rice for 10 minutes, refresh under cold running water, and drain thoroughly.
3 Heat the oil, lightly sauté the onion until it is pale in color, add the garlic and bacon, and cook gently for 2–3 minutes more.
4 Chop the inner small cabbage leaves. Put the onion and bacon mixture in a large bowl and add the other ingredients for the stuffing: the chopped cabbage leaves, rice, tomatoes, peas, sausage meat, hyssop. Season well and mix together thoroughly.
5 Heat the oven to 350°F/180°C.
6 Line a bowl with a piece of cheesecloth and spread over it the large leaves, to reconstitute the cabbage. Put the stuffing in the center and fold the leaves over it to form a ball. Tie up the cheesecloth to keep it in shape.
7 Transfer the cabbage to an ovenproof casserole, add enough stock to fill it by two thirds, cover tightly, and bake in the oven for 2 hours.
8 To serve, lift out the cabbage with a slotted spoon. Remove the cheesecloth. Put the cabbage in a large bowl. Keep it warm while you boil the cooking liquor to reduce it by half. Garnish with a few hyssop sprigs and serve the sauce separately.
KCal 405 P 12 C 25g S 701mg SFA 10g UFA 18g

BUTTERNUT SQUASH WITH TARRAGON

Serves 2–3.

INGREDIENTS

1 butternut squash, weighing approximately 1lb (500g)
4 tbsp butter
black pepper
1½ tbsp chopped fresh tarragon or 2 tsp crumbled dried

PREPARATION

1 Peel and halve the squash, remove the seeds and fibrous parts, and cube the flesh. Melt the butter in a pan. Cook the squash over low heat, covered, for 10–15 minutes. Alternatively, microwave the unpeeled squash halves: put butter in the cavities, cover with plastic wrap, and cook for 10 minutes.
2 Purée the squash, season with pepper, and stir in the tarragon. If necessary, add more butter. It is good served with pork noisettes (see page 101).
KCal 299 P 3g C 17g S 234mg SFA 16g UFA 7g

LENTILS FLAVORED WITH HERBS, INDIAN STYLE

The use of oil or butter, scented with herbs or spices, to finish a dish of lentils is basic to Indian cooking. Vary the herbs to your taste, but use enough; lentils can absorb a lot of flavoring.

INGREDIENTS

1 cup (250g) small green or brown lentils
2 bay leaves
1 medium onion, whole
6 tbsp sunflower or olive oil
2–3 tbsp chopped cilantro
1 tbsp chopped cilantro root
2–3 tbsp chopped basil, preferably anise or Thai
2 tbsp chopped mint, preferably Tashkent or lemon
salt and black pepper
2 tbsp chopped holy basil

PREPARATION

1 Cook the lentils in unsalted water with the bay leaves and onion until tender, about 25 minutes. Drain thoroughly, discarding the onion and bay.
2 Heat the oil in a large pan and cook all the herbs, except the holy basil, for 3–4 minutes.
3 Stir in the cooked lentils, heat through, and season with salt and pepper. Add the holy basil. Serve with rice as part of a vegetarian meal or to accompany meat or fish.
KCal 415 P 17g C 35g S 14mg SFA 3g UFA 20g

CELERY STAMPPOT

Stamppot is a traditional Dutch winter dish of potato mashed with another vegetable or with apples. Leeks, carrots, kale, cabbage, and onions are commonly used; this version uses cutting celery. It is a strong-flavored herb that in parts of northern Europe is used to some extent as a garnish, as parsley is used elsewhere. I prefer it cooked rather than raw. If you want to try a different herb, select something with a clear flavor such as cilantro, savory, or lovage.

INGREDIENTS

*4 large potatoes
about 3½ cups (100g) cutting celery
8 tbsp butter
3–4 tbsp plain yogurt
black pepper and salt*

PREPARATION

1 Boil the potatoes in salted water, then drain.
2 Remove the thick celery stalks and coarsely chop the leaves in a food processor. Sauté briefly in half the butter, then add them to the potatoes and mash, adding more butter as necessary.
3 Add the yogurt. (I find this helps bring out the taste of the celery while tempering its bitterness.)
4 Season with pepper, and a little salt if necessary. Reheat and serve.
KCal 467 P 8g C 53 S 272mg SFA 17g UFA 7g

MORELS WITH GARLIC AND HERBS

This is a lovely late spring dish; the fresh morels, mild new garlic, and herbs all appear at the same time and the flavors blend beautifully.

INGREDIENTS

*1lb (500g) fresh morels
7 tbsp (100g) butter
3 new garlic cloves, crushed and coarsely chopped
2 tbsp chopped chervil
1 tbsp chopped summer savory
2 tbsp chopped basil or parsley
1 tbsp chopped tarragon*

PREPARATION

1 Halve the morels lengthwise. Wash well in salted water and drain. Stew gently in butter for 10 minutes. Add the garlic. Cook for 5 minutes.
2 Arrange the morels in a serving dish and stir in the mixed herbs. Serve at once.
KCal 209 P 3g C 2g S 197mg SFA 14g UFA 6g

STUFFED ZUCCHINI FLOWERS

This Greek dish must be made with freshly picked zucchini or pumpkin flowers, before they begin to fade and crumple. The flowers are often available in season from specialty stores and farmers' markets. Sometimes they are sold with a small zucchini still attached. A little grated zucchini can be added to the stuffing if you wish. Serves 6.

INGREDIENTS

*2–3 tbsp olive oil
2 garlic cloves, finely chopped
1 bunch scallions or Welsh onion tops,
finely chopped
1¼ cups (200g) long-grain rice
2 tbsp tomato paste
1 tsp sugar
salt and black pepper
pinch of cinnamon
3 tbsp chopped flat-leaf parsley
1 tbsp chopped mint
2 tbsp chopped fennel
24 zucchini flowers
1 egg, beaten
lemon juice, to taste*

PREPARATION

1 Heat the oil and sauté the garlic and scallions until soft. Stir in the rice and tomato paste and season with sugar, salt, pepper, and cinnamon. Add the parsley, mint, and fennel, and make sure that all the ingredients are evenly distributed through the mixture.
2 Fill each flower carefully, folding the tops of the petals over the stuffing (see opposite). Put them in a large shallow skillet in which they will fit in a single layer, cover with water, and bring slowly to a boil. Reduce the heat and simmer for about 25 minutes, until the rice is cooked. Check them occasionally to see if more water is needed. Remove the pan from the heat and let stand for a few minutes.
3 Lift out the flowers with a slotted spoon. Reduce the cooking liquid a little if necessary: there should be about 1 cup (250ml). Remove the pan from the heat and whisk in the beaten egg to thicken it further. Add lemon juice to taste, pour over the zucchini flowers, and serve at room temperature, the Greek way, as a first course or to accompany roast lamb.
KCal 210 P 6g C 32g S 33mg SFA 1g UFA 5g

STUFFING ZUCCHINI FLOWERS

1 *Gently fold back the petals of the zucchini flowers.*

2 *Spoon in the stuffing, carefully pushing it down to the base. Do not overfill or the flowers may burst when the rice swells during cooking.*

3 *Fold the tops of the petals over the stuffing. The flowers have a slightly elastic texture that should keep the mixture securely wrapped inside.*

New Potatoes with Fenugreek

This classic north Indian dish is made with very tiny potatoes. If you cannot get really small ones, use new potatoes cut in half or quartered.

INGREDIENTS

about 8 cups (250g) fresh fenugreek leaves or
2 tbsp dried (see Iranian Lamb Stew on page 96)
4–5 tbsp sunflower or peanut oil
1 tsp cumin seeds
1 green chili, chopped (optional)
½ tsp turmeric
1lb (500g) new potatoes
½ tsp garam masala
salt
1 tbsp lemon juice or more, to taste

PREPARATION

1 Discard any fenugreek stems, whether using fresh or dried. Wash fresh leaves in several changes of water and chop them. Rinse dried leaves.
2 Heat the oil in a heavy, wide pan and add the cumin seeds. When they change color, after 20 seconds or so, add the chili and turmeric, stir, and put in the potatoes. Cook for 5 minutes over medium heat, stirring constantly.
3 Add the fenugreek leaves, lower the heat, and cook for 4–5 minutes longer, still stirring, until the greens are wilted. Sprinkle with garam masala and a little salt.
4 Cover the pan tightly and leave on very low heat for 20–25 minutes, until the potatoes are cooked. Stir gently once or twice. Usually no liquid is added but, if the potatoes become too dry, sprinkle them with a tablespoon or two of water.
5 When cooked, add lemon juice to taste and serve.
KCal 241 P 5g C 23g S 160mg SFA 2g UFA 13g

Spinach and Herb Tart

INGREDIENTS

about 5 cups (150g) spinach
about 5 cups (150g) sorrel
about 5 cups (150g) flat-leaf parsley
about 5 cups (150g) chervil
1 lettuce heart
a few borage leaves
1 bunch scallions or Welsh onion tops
3 eggs
1¼ cups (300ml) heavy cream
4 tbsp fresh bread crumbs
salt and black pepper
½lb (250g) phyllo pastry
4 tbsp butter, melted

PREPARATION

1 Boil the spinach, sorrel, and other herbs in plenty of water for a few minutes. Drain and press to squeeze out all the water, then coarsely chop.
2 Chop the scallions and stir into the herb mixture. Whisk the eggs lightly. Heat the cream with the bread crumbs and stir until it thickens slightly. Stir in the eggs and herbs and season.
3 Heat the oven to 350°F/180°C. Put a 10in (25cm) loose-bottomed tart pan on a baking sheet and surround it with a roll of crumpled foil to support the pastry.
4 To make the tart case, use 2 sheets of phyllo at a time. Keep the others under a damp cloth. Brush the sheets lightly with butter and put them in the pan. Place the sheets over one another at different angles to ensure the base is evenly covered and the corners hang over the edges of the pan at intervals.
5 Pour in the filling and shake the pan to distribute it evenly. Bake for about 40 minutes. Serve the tart either hot or warm.
KCal 577 P 18g C 51g S 546mg SFA 19g UFA 12g

Moorish Eggplants

INGREDIENTS

2 medium eggplants
2 garlic cloves, crushed
handful of flat-leaf parsley leaves
handful of basil leaves, including cinnamon
or holy basil if available
8 salted anchovy fillets
1 cup (100g) walnuts
5 tbsp red wine vinegar
approximately ⅔ cup (150ml) olive oil
pinch of cayenne or ¼ tsp red pepper flakes

PREPARATION

1 Cut the eggplants in quarters lengthwise and boil in salted water for 10–15 minutes, depending on size. Drain and plunge into a bowl of ice water. Leave for a few hours until the pieces become firm.
2 Put the garlic, parsley, basil, anchovies, walnuts, and vinegar in a food processor and blend to a thick paste, scraping down the sides several times. While the machine is running, add enough oil to make a thick sauce. Season with cayenne.
3 Dry the eggplants on paper towels, arrange on a dish, and cover with sauce. Refrigerate overnight.
KCal 568 P 8g C 5g S 407mg SFA 7g UFA 35g

STUFFED ARTICHOKES

Turkish cooking has a whole family of meatless dishes called "olive oil dishes." Leeks, celeriac, eggplants, and beans are all delicious prepared this way, with or without stuffing. Illustrated on page 110. Serves 6.

INGREDIENTS

3 lemons
2 tbsp all-purpose flour
6 medium artichokes
salt
3 tbsp olive oil
1 tsp sugar
Stuffing
6 tbsp olive oil
3 medium onions, finely chopped
1 tbsp unsalted pistachio or pine nuts
⅓ cup (60g) long-grain rice
salt and black pepper
1 tsp ground allspice
1 cup (30g) chopped flat-leaf parsley
1 cup (30g) chopped dill
1 cup (30g) chopped mint
lemon slices and dill, to garnish

PREPARATION

1 Mix together the juice of 1 lemon and the flour with 1 cup (250ml) water in a bowl and keep nearby as you prepare the artichokes.
2 Cut off the artichoke stems and outer leaves. Bend back the inner leaves and snap them near the bottom, leaving the fleshy part attached to the base. The fresher the artichokes, the easier they will snap; cut the leaves if necessary. Slice off the innermost leaves just above the base and scoop out completely the fuzzy chokes. As you clean each artichoke, rub it with half a lemon sprinkled with salt to prevent discoloration and put it in the lemon-flour-water mixture.
3 To make the stuffing, heat the oil in a heavy pan and sauté the onions. Add the nuts and cook until they turn golden, then stir in the rice. Season with salt, pepper, and allspice and sauté for 5 minutes longer. Add ⅔ cup (150ml) boiling water, cover, and simmer for 10–15 minutes, or until the rice is almost tender and the water has been absorbed. Take the pan off the heat and stir in the chopped parsley, dill, and mint.
4 Remove the artichokes from the liquid, setting it to one side, and stuff them with the rice and nut mixture. Arrange them in a single layer in a flame-proof casserole. Add the reserved lemon-flour-water mixture and 3 tablespoons olive oil, pouring it between the vegetables and the side of the pan.

5 Sprinkle over the sugar. Put a sheet of moistened waxed paper over the artichokes and put on the lid. Cook over medium heat for 10 minutes. Reduce the heat to very low and simmer for 1 hour. If you prefer, cook them in the oven at 350°F/180°C.
6 Let the artichokes cool in the casserole. Lift them out onto a platter and serve cold, garnished with lemon slices and dill.
KCal 323 P 6g C 22g S 112mg SFA 4g UFA 20g

GRATIN OF FENNEL

A good main dish for a vegetarian meal, or an accompaniment to roast meat or baked fish. Illustrated on page 111.

INGREDIENTS

4 bulbs Florence fennel
6 tbsp olive oil
1 medium onion, sliced
2 garlic cloves, sliced
¾lb (400g) tomatoes, peeled, seeded, and chopped
1 tbsp chopped winter savory
2 tbsp chopped lemon balm
salt and black pepper
½ cup (125ml) dry white wine
5 tbsp coarse dried bread crumbs

PREPARATION

1 Remove the outer leaves of the fennel and slice the bulbs thickly. Heat 4 tablespoons of the olive oil and sauté the onion and garlic over low heat. Add the fennel and let the pieces color lightly, turning them from time to time with a wooden spoon. Do not let any of the vegetables burn.
2 Heat the oven to 400°F/200°C.
3 Add the tomatoes and herbs, season with salt and pepper, and simmer for 5 minutes.
4 Transfer the vegetables to a gratin dish. Deglaze the pan with wine over high heat. Pour the wine over the fennel. Scatter bread crumbs on top and drizzle over the remaining oil. Bake for 20 minutes.
KCal 318 P 4g C 19g S 146mg SFA 3g UFA 19g

*Purslane and
Spinach Salad
(see page 112)*

*Stuffed Artichokes
(see previous page)*

Gratin of Fennel
(see page 109)

SALADS

A bouquet of fresh herbs is essential when composing a salad: even a few parsley leaves will enliven the flavors. Add herbs to vinaigrettes and to cream and yogurt dressings, or use them to scent the oil or butter for croutons. Some salad herbs, such as arugula and dandelion, are excellent with fruit; a final scattering of flowers produces a combination that is hard to resist.

PURSLANE AND SPINACH SALAD

Try to get a piece of feta cheese that is not too salty; some salt can be drawn out by soaking the cheese in water for a few hours. Illustrated on page 110.

INGREDIENTS

4 cups (100g) young spinach leaves
4 cups (100g) purslane sprigs
handful of young nasturtium leaves or salad burnet
¼lb (100g) feta cheese, drained weight
nasturtium flowers
2 tbsp walnut oil
3 tbsp olive oil
2 tbsp herb vinegar
black pepper

PREPARATION

1 Arrange the spinach, purslane, and nasturtium leaves in a salad bowl. Crumble the feta cheese over them and top with the nasturtium flowers.
2 Whisk the walnut and olive oil with the vinegar to make a dressing and season with pepper. Spoon it over the salad.
KCal 248 P 6g C 2g S 405mg SFA 7g UFA 17g

MINT, CARROT, AND HAMBURG PARSLEY SALAD

This recipe comes from Culinary and Salad Herbs *by Eleanour Sinclair Rohde, published in 1940. The original recipe calls for no oil, but a tablespoonful may be added. Lovage is a good alternative to mint, but use less, about 2 cups (60g). I have also made the salad with grated celeriac instead of Hamburg parsley, to good effect. Remember to grate white roots at the last minute to avoid discoloration. Serves 2.*

INGREDIENTS

1 small onion, finely sliced
4 cups (100g) mint leaves
2 heaping tbsp grated carrot
2 heaping tbsp grated Hamburg parsley root
lemon juice, to taste
salt and black pepper

PREPARATION

1 Pound the onion with the mint or blend briefly in a food processor. Stir in the carrot and parsley root.
2 Dress with lemon juice, salt, and pepper.
KCal 51 P 3g C 9g S 32mg SFA neg UFA neg

GREEN BEAN AND MUSHROOM SALAD

INGREDIENTS

½lb (200g) green beans, trimmed
¼lb (100g) mushrooms
3 tbsp sunflower oil
2 tbsp light soy sauce
2 tbsp rice or wine vinegar
salt and black pepper
a few Chinese chives, cut into short lengths
2–3 rao ram leaves or a few cilantro or water celery leaves, shredded

PREPARATION

1 Cook the green beans in boiling water until barely tender, then drain. Quarter the mushrooms.
2 Heat a wok, and when it is very hot, pour in 2 tablespoons of the oil. Add the mushrooms and stir-fry them quickly, then add the beans and stir-fry for 1 minute longer.
3 Whisk together the remaining oil, soy sauce, and vinegar. Season the dressing with salt and pepper.
4 Put the vegetables in a bowl and scatter over the herbs. Pour on the dressing and toss the salad so that the mushrooms and beans are well coated.
KCal 123 P 2g C 3g S 433mg SFA 1g UFA 10g

PEAR AND RASPBERRY SALAD

*This recipe comes from Angelo Lancellotti of
the renowned Da Lancellotti restaurant in Soliera,
near Modena in Italy. Illustrated above.*

INGREDIENTS

4 tbsp raspberries
3 ripe pears
handful of arugula leaves, coarsely chopped
1–2 sprigs of tarragon, finely chopped
1–2 tbsp virgin olive oil
1 tbsp balsamic vinegar
violet and borage flowers

PREPARATION

1 Squash the raspberries with a fork. Slice the
pears at the last moment to prevent discoloration.
2 Mix the herbs and fruit, letting the raspberries
coat the pears. Add the olive oil, then the vinegar,
and toss. Scatter the flowers on top and serve.
KCal 71 P 1g C 9g S 4mg SFA 1g UFA 3g

APPLE, DANDELION, AND NASTURTIUM SALAD

Another original salad from Angelo Lancellotti.

INGREDIENTS

3 sweet firm apples
lemon juice
small bunch of chives
large handful of dandelion leaves
a few marjoram sprigs, coarsely chopped
2–3 tbsp virgin olive oil
1 tbsp balsamic vinegar
nasturtium and marjoram flowers

PREPARATION

1 Slice the apples and paint them with lemon juice
to prevent discoloration. Cut the chives, and
dandelion leaves if necessary, into short lengths.
Combine all the herbs with the apple slices.
2 Dress with oil and vinegar and add the flowers.
KCal 119 P 2g C 11g S 6mg SFA 1g UFA 6g

PARSLEY AND TAHINI SALAD

An extremely versatile dish from Lebanon. The salad is an excellent accompaniment to roast meats and hard-cooked eggs. Tahini is an oily paste made from crushed sesame seeds.

INGREDIENTS

about 12 cups (350g) flat-leaf parsley
1–2 garlic cloves
salt
1 cup (200ml) tahini
juice of 1–2 lemons
4 tbsp water

PREPARATION

1 Cut or pluck the leaves from the parsley and discard the stems. Keep the leaves whole.
2 Crush the garlic with a little salt. Mix the tahini, lemon juice, and water to make the dressing. Add the garlic. Use more salt or lemon juice if you wish.
3 Put the parsley leaves in a serving bowl. Pour over the dressing, mix well, and serve.
KCal 335 P 12g C 3g S 136mg SFA 4g UFA 24g

VARIATIONS

With a little less parsley and tahini and more water, this makes a good dip to serve with bread or raw vegetables. With even less parsley and equivalent amounts of tahini and water (about ½ cup/100ml), it makes a fine sauce for chicken or grilled fish. Experiment to find the balance you prefer.

DAIKON AND KIWIFRUIT SALAD

Illustrated on page 58.

INGREDIENTS

1 daikon, weighing about ½lb (250g)
1 tbsp lemon juice
3 kiwifruit, ripe but still firm
4 tbsp sunflower oil
2 tsp sesame oil
2 tbsp rice or cider vinegar
2 tsp light soy sauce
salt
1 tbsp dry-roasted sesame seeds (see page 93)
a few purple and green basil leaves or perilla leaves

PREPARATION

1 Peel the daikon, slice thin, and sprinkle with lemon juice to prevent discoloration. Peel and slice the kiwifruit fairly thin.
2 Make a dressing with the oils, vinegar, soy sauce, and salt. Arrange the radish and kiwifruit on a serving plate and scatter over the sesame seeds. Spoon over the dressing. Top with torn basil or perilla leaves.
KCal 217 P 2g C 8g S 211mg SFA 3g UFA 17g

FAVA BEAN SALAD WITH PROSCIUTTO

A pleasant salad in which several herbs would work — calamint, chives, lemon balm, or salad burnet. Using hazelnut oil and herb vinegar would be another way of making subtle flavor changes. Illustrated on page 59.

INGREDIENTS

3 cups (350g) small fava beans, shelled
4 tbsp olive oil
½lb (200g) red cherry tomatoes, halved
4 slices prosciutto, cut into julienne strips
1 tbsp sherry or cider vinegar
salt and black pepper
1 tbsp chopped fresh marjoram

PREPARATION

1 Cook the beans in boiling water for 3–5 minutes, until just tender. Drain and sprinkle with 1 tablespoon of the oil, and let cool.
2 Make a vinaigrette from the remaining oil and the vinegar. Season with salt and pepper.
3 Mix the vegetables with the prosciutto in a shallow dish and dress with the vinaigrette. Scatter over the marjoram and serve.
KCal 228 P 10g C 8g S 321mg SFA 3g UFA 14g

RED PEPPER SALAD WITH OLIVES AND ANCHOVIES

If possible, use a mixture of black, purple, and dark green bruised-looking olives, to add variety of taste and color to the salad. Illustrated on page 58.

INGREDIENTS

4 red peppers
large handful of cilantro leaves
4 tbsp olive oil
2 tbsp red wine vinegar
½ cup (100g) olives
8 anchovy fillets

PREPARATION

1 Roast the peppers over a gas flame or under a broiler until charred all over. Put in a heavy plastic bag for 10 minutes. This makes them easier to peel, as does holding them under running cold water. Cut the peeled flesh into strips.
2 Coarsely chop the cilantro, but keep a few leaves whole. Mix the oil and vinegar to make a vinaigrette.
3 Mix the peppers, olives, and chopped cilantro in a bowl, arrange the anchovies and whole cilantro on top, and dress with the vinaigrette.
KCal 272 P 6g C 16g S 971mg SFA 3g UFA 15g

MANGO, MINT, AND SHRIMP SALAD

Illustrated on page 58.

INGREDIENTS

2 ripe mangoes, peeled
4 tbsp light cream
4 tbsp heavy cream
½–1 tsp garam masala
1–2 tbsp lime juice
20 jumbo shrimp or tiger prawns, cooked, peeled, and deveined
3–4 sprigs of mint

PREPARATION

1 Slice the mangoes. Reserve their juices, together with any flesh adhering to the pits, for the dressing.
2 Blend together the light and heavy cream, garam masala, and lime juice. Very finely chop any bits of leftover mango flesh and add them to the dressing with the mango juice. Adjust the quantities of garam masala and lime juice to taste.
3 Arrange the fruit and shrimp on a serving plate. Spoon the dressing over the salad. Shred the mint leaves and scatter them over the top.
KCal 188 P 10g C 14g S 110mg SFA 6g UFA 3g

HERB AND FLOWER SALAD

Most green salads benefit from the addition of herbs, and you can also make a salad largely composed of herb leaves. Choose a mixture of strong and milder flavored leaves from angelica, anise, anise hyssop, arugula, balm, the basils, bergamot, borage, burnet, caraway, chervil, chives, dandelion, hyssop, lovage, marsh mallow, the mints, mint-scented marigold, purslane, a small leaf or two of rue, sorrel, and sweet cicely. Garnish with herb flowers such as bergamot, borage, marigold, micromeria, nasturtium, rosemary, sage, thyme, or violets. Dress with a vinaigrette made with an herb vinegar or oil, or try this creamy dressing. (Illustrated on page 59.)

INGREDIENTS

Creamy Dressing
2 hard-cooked egg yolks
1 tsp Dijon mustard
black pepper and salt
6 tbsp (90ml) cream
1 tbsp vinegar, preferably herb vinegar

PREPARATION

1 Sieve the yolks and add the mustard, pepper, and a little salt. Mix in the cream, then stir in the vinegar.
2 Pour the dressing over the salad and toss.
Nutritional values for total amount of dressing:
KCal 288 P 8g C 4g S 404mg SFA 13g UFA 11g

PASTA AND GRAINS

Grains are neutral and absorb flavors readily, so they benefit greatly from the addition of herbs. Pasta sauces and fillings are improved by a handful of herbs; rice flecked with green looks beautiful and can have a delicate or pungent taste depending on the leaves chosen. Less widely used grains such as barley or bulgur wheat are also enhanced by herbs, although in their traditional cultures these may not be their regular companions.

LINGUINE WITH HERB SAUCE

The herbs for this sauce can be varied to include whatever is available, but they must be fresh. Aim for a harmonious blend of strong and more delicate flavors.

INGREDIENTS

1 young angelica leaf
4 stalks basil
4 stalks summer savory
2 stalks tarragon
1 stalk anise hyssop
2 young stalks lovage
3 stalks marjoram
2 sprays sweet cicely
6 sorrel leaves
handful of chervil or parsley
8–10 tbsp (120–150ml) virgin olive oil
3 tbsp chopped scallions or Welsh onion
3–4 tbsp fresh bread crumbs
1lb (500g) linguine
black pepper
freshly grated Parmesan, to serve

PREPARATION

1 Remove any thick stems from the herbs and then chop them all coarsely.
2 Heat 2 tablespoons of the oil in a pan and sauté the scallions and bread crumbs until crisp. Put the remaining oil in a large bowl and add all the herbs.
3 Meanwhile, bring a large pan of salted water to a boil and cook the linguine according to the package directions. Drain well and toss it in the oil and herb mixture.
4 Season with black pepper and scatter over the onion and bread crumbs. Serve with some grated Parmesan to sprinkle over.
KCal 812 P 23g C 101g S 234mg SFA 8g UFA 28g

FARFALLE WITH ANGELICA AND PANCETTA

Farfalle, or pasta bows, are ideal with this sauce, but you can also use other shaped pasta such as shells or corkscrewlike fusilli. The angelica stems should be no thicker than a pencil, or they may be tough and too strongly flavored.

INGREDIENTS

2 shallots, chopped
2 tbsp butter
4 thin stalks angelica
¼lb (100g) pancetta or smoked lean bacon
¾lb (400g) farfalle
1 tbsp hyssop leaves
⅔ cup (150ml) light cream
salt and black pepper
1 tbsp olive oil

PREPARATION

1 Put the shallots in a pan to soften in the butter over low heat. Cut the angelica stems into ½in (1cm) lengths and the pancetta into small cubes. Add them to the shallots and cook for 3–4 minutes longer.
2 Bring a pan of salted water to a boil for the farfalle and cook the pasta according to the package directions.
3 Add the hyssop and cream to the shallots, angelica, and pancetta. Reduce the heat and cook, stirring constantly, until the cream is almost boiling. Add a little salt and lots of pepper. Cover and keep warm at the side of the stove.
4 When the pasta is cooked – it should remain *al dente* – drain well and put it in a serving bowl. Toss with the olive oil, then pour over the sauce and serve.
KCal 555 P 18g C 21g S 612mg SFA 10g UFA 9g

FETTUCCINE WITH SHRIMP AND TOMATO SAUCE

Tuna or swordfish, cut into cubes, makes an excellent alternative to shrimp. Cook 8–10oz (250–300g) in the sauce for 8–10 minutes.

INGREDIENTS

3 tbsp olive oil
20 large uncooked shrimp, peeled and deveined
3 garlic cloves, finely sliced
2 tsp chopped lemon thyme
1 cup (200ml) tomato passata (comes in a box)
salt and black pepper
12 green olives, pitted and halved
1 red pepper, peeled, seeded, and sliced (see page 102)
¾lb (400g) fresh fettuccine
large handful of basil, shredded

PREPARATION

1 Heat 2 tablespoons of the oil in a skillet and cook the shrimp for 2–3 minutes, until they curl and turn pink. Remove them and set aside. Add the garlic to the pan and cook over low heat until soft, but do not let it burn. Meanwhile, heat a large pan of salted water for the fettuccine.

2 Add the thyme to the garlic, then pour in the passata and season with salt and pepper. Simmer for a few minutes, then add the olives and red pepper. When the pasta water comes to a boil, reduce the heat under the sauce so that it barely bubbles and add the shrimp.

3 Cook the fettuccine until *al dente*, then drain well. Put it in a serving bowl and toss with the remaining oil. Toss the basil into the sauce, pour it over the pasta, and serve.

KCal 482 P 22g C 59g S 569mg SFA 3g UFA 14g

PASTA CON LE SARDE
Pasta with sardines

*This is a traditional Sicilian dish, particularly popular
in Palermo. The Sicilians use wild fennel, but garden
fennel works well. The sardines must be fresh. Serves 6.*

INGREDIENTS

*1½lb (750g) fresh sardines
¾lb (400g) green or bronze fennel
½ cup (100g) raisins
6 saffron threads
½ cup (125ml) olive oil
1 large onion, finely chopped
6 anchovy fillets
¾ cup (100g) pine nuts
1lb (500g) macaroni or bucatini*

PREPARATION

1 Clean the sardines by scraping off the scales
from tail to head with the back of a knife. Rinse in
cold water, then slit along the length of the belly
and take out the innards. Cut off the heads and tails
and rinse again. To fillet them, open each fish by
pressing your thumb along the backbone to loosen
it and free the flesh. Lift out the backbone together
with the smaller bones.

2 Remove the thick stalks from the fennel and boil
the leaves for 8–10 minutes in plenty of salted
water. Drain, reserving the liquid to cook the
pasta. Let the fennel cool and coarsely chop it.

3 Plump the raisins in hot water for 10 minutes.
Crush the saffron in a little water.

4 Heat 2 tablespoons of oil in a large pan and cook
the onion until golden. Add the anchovy fillets and
cook until softened. Stir in the pine nuts, drained
raisins, and saffron water. Cover and simmer for
10–15 minutes. Add a little water if necessary.

5 Heat 3 tablespoons of oil in a second pan, put in
half the sardines, crush with the back of a wooden
spoon, and cook to a paste, stirring frequently. Add
the fennel and cook for a few minutes longer, then
combine with the onion mixture.

6 Wipe out the pan, add 3 tablespoons of oil, and
cook the remaining sardine fillets on both sides
until golden. They are rather fragile, so be careful
when turning them. Drain on paper towels.

7 Heat the oven to 375°F/190°C. Bring the
fennel water to a boil again and cook the pasta
until *al dente*. Drain and toss with the sauce. Put
half the macaroni into an ovenproof dish, cover
with a layer of sardines, and top with the rest of
the pasta. Cover the dish and bake for 15 minutes.
Serve hot or cold.

KCal 775 P 28g C 79g S 300mg SFA 6g UFA 32g

Olive oil

Saffron

Raisins

Fennel

Sardines

Onion

Anchovy fillets

Pine nuts

Macaroni

LEEK AND HERB RISOTTO

The herbs for this aromatic risotto can be varied to suit your own taste, but make sure you have a balance between the lighter and stronger tasting kinds.

INGREDIENTS

4 young leeks
4 tbsp butter
1 garlic clove, chopped
1 tbsp chopped parsley
1 tbsp chopped sage
1 tbsp chopped sweet cicely
1 tbsp chopped marjoram
1 tsp chopped hyssop
1 tsp chopped rosemary
1 tsp chopped thyme
2¼ cups (475g) carnaroli or arborio rice
approximately 4½ cups (1¼ liters) hot chicken or vegetable stock
12 green olives, pitted and chopped
1 tbsp chopped basil
½ cup (30g) freshly grated Parmesan
salt and black pepper

PREPARATION

1 Clean the leeks and slice them fairly fine. Melt half the butter in a large heavy pan and cook the leeks and garlic over low heat for about 5 minutes, stirring frequently.
2 Put in all the herbs (except the chopped basil), then let the flavors blend for a minute or two. Add the rice and stir so that all the grains are coated with butter.
3 Raise the heat to medium and pour in a ladleful of hot stock. Stir constantly to ensure the rice does not stick to the pan and the liquid is distributed evenly. When this has been absorbed, add another ladleful of stock, keep stirring, and continue in this way until the rice is tender. It should have a creamy consistency.
4 Keep testing the rice after it has been cooking for 20 minutes to see how much more stock is needed; different types of rice absorb liquid at different rates. During the last few minutes of cooking, take care not to add too much. (You may not need to use the full quantity.) Keep stirring regularly so that the rice does not stick to the bottom of the pan.
5 When the rice is cooked, stir in the remaining butter, the olives, basil, and Parmesan. Season with a little salt if necessary, and generously with black pepper. Serve at once.
KCal 663 P15g C 108g S 542mg SFA 11g UFA 9g

IRANIAN RICE WITH HERBS

This is a beautiful dish, traditionally served at the Noo Rooz, or New Year, festival, which is celebrated in March and marks the beginning of spring. Fresh herbs give a good clean flavor, but Iranian shops sell large bags of dried herbs specially mixed for cooking rice. They are exceptionally fragrant. You will need only 2–2½oz (60–70g) dried herbs to season 2½ cups (500g) rice. Serves 4–6.

INGREDIENTS

2½ cups (500g) basmati rice
salt
2 bunches scallions or 1 bunch scallions and 1 bunch chives
about 4 cups (100g) parsley
about 4 cups (100g) cilantro
about 4 cups (100g) dill
7 tbsp (100g) butter

PREPARATION

1 Soak the rice for several hours in salted water, then drain. Add 1 tablespoon of salt to 10 cups (2½ liters) of water, bring to a boil, and add the rice. Boil, uncovered, for 3–4 minutes, stirring from time to time with a wooden fork. The rice should still be quite firm. Drain and rinse with lukewarm water.
2 Chop the scallions fine. Remove any large stems from the herbs and finely chop them all. Mix the herbs with the scallions.
3 Rinse the pan and add half the butter. Let it melt, add 2–3 tablespoons of water, and when hot, cover the bottom of the pan with a layer of rice. Spread over a thinner layer of herb mixture. Repeat the layers, finishing with rice, and mound the layers into a pyramid.
4 Melt the remaining butter and pour it over the rice. Poke a hole down through the center with the handle of a wooden spoon. Cover with a cloth, then the pan lid, and steam over very low heat for 30 minutes. The rice can be left longer, and will keep hot for 20 minutes or so after the heat has been turned off, provided the cloth and lid are left in place and not disturbed.
5 To serve, toss the rice with a fork to blend in the herbs and heap up in a serving dish. A crisp golden crust should have formed on the bottom of the pan. Remove it with a spatula and serve as an accompaniment. The rice goes well with pan-fried fish and with most meats.
KCal 694 P 13g C 110g S 315mg SFA 15g UFA 9g

BAKED POLENTA WITH MUSHROOMS

INGREDIENTS

1 cup (150g) polenta (cornmeal)
4 tbsp chopped flat-leaf parsley
2 tbsp chopped oregano
4 tbsp olive oil
½ cup (20g) dried porcini or other mushrooms
1 onion, chopped
1 carrot, chopped
1 garlic clove, chopped
10oz (300g) fresh mushrooms, sliced
¾lb (400g) tomatoes, peeled, seeded, and chopped
salt and black pepper
½ cup (60g) freshly grated Parmesan
4 tbsp butter

PREPARATION

1 Bring 2½ cups (600ml) lightly salted water to a boil and add the polenta, stirring hard. When it comes back to a boil, reduce the heat and cook for 20 minutes, stirring from time to time.

2 Lightly sauté half the parsley and oregano in a tablespoon of oil and stir into the cooked polenta. Spoon it into a shallow rectangular baking pan to make a layer ¾in (1.5cm) thick. Let cool.

3 Soak the dried mushrooms in some warm water. Heat the oven to 350°F/180°C.

4 Heat the remaining oil. Sauté the onion, carrot, and garlic until the onion is soft. Put in the fresh mushrooms and tomatoes. Season and add the rest of the oregano. Cook for 10 minutes: the mushrooms should still be firm, but have given off their liquid.

5 Drain the dried mushrooms, chop them, and add to the sauce. Cook for 5 minutes longer. Stir in the rest of the parsley.

6 Cut the polenta into squares and put a layer into a buttered ovenproof dish. Spread a layer of sauce over it and about half the Parmesan, then dot with butter. Repeat the layers, dotting the top liberally with butter. Bake in the oven for 20–25 minutes, until the top is browned. Serve with a green salad.
KCal 527 P 13g C 41g S 354g SFA 14g UFA 19g

RIGATONI WITH HERB SAUCE

INGREDIENTS

¾lb (400g) rigatoni or pasta bows
½ cup (100ml) olive oil
2 tbsp butter
2 anchovy fillets, finely chopped
2 garlic cloves
2 sage leaves
5–6 mint leaves
7–8 large basil leaves
leaves from 1 sprig rosemary
leaves from 1 sprig thyme
leaves from 1 sprig savory
handful of chervil
handful of flat-leaf parsley
salt and black pepper
freshly grated Parmesan, to serve (optional)

PREPARATION

1 Bring a large pot of water to a boil and cook the pasta as directed on the package, then drain.

2 Heat the oil and butter in a large pan and gently cook the anchovies, stirring frequently, until they have melted and thickened the oil and butter.

3 Finely chop the garlic and all the herbs and add to the anchovies. Stir them gently over low heat for 3–4 minutes to release their aroma.

4 Stir in the pasta and season to taste. Scatter over some Parmesan when serving, if you wish.
KCal 647 P 14g C 77g S 175mg SFA 8g UFA 24g

ELINOR'S COUSCOUS AND VEGETABLE SALAD

INGREDIENTS

1½ cups (300g) chickpeas, soaked overnight
2½ cups (500g) couscous
approximately 5–7 tbsp (75–105ml) olive oil
10oz (300g) mushrooms, quartered
4 zucchini, halved lengthwise and sliced into half-rounds
6 scallions, sliced
small bunch of cilantro, chopped
salt and black pepper

PREPARATION

1 Cook the chickpeas in unsalted water until tender, 1–1½ hours, depending on their age. If you are in a hurry, use canned, draining and rinsing them well. Cook the couscous according to the package directions, dress with a little olive oil, and let cool.

2 Sauté the mushrooms in 2–3 tablespoons of the oil. Then sauté the zucchini separately in another 2 tablespoons of oil.

3 Spread the couscous in the bottom of a serving dish and season with salt and pepper. Arrange the vegetables on top and scatter over the cilantro.
KCal 900 P 34g C 137g S 49mg SFA 3g UFA 23g

DESSERTS

The use of herbs in desserts and cakes is perhaps unexpected, but scented geraniums, lavender, and bay have a delicate yet persistent perfume that is ideal for custards and ices. Other herbs, among them mint and tarragon, have a clean taste that adds a refreshing touch of sharpness to a sweet dish, and a few – sweet cicely, lemon verbena, and lemon balm – marry well with fruit. Herb sugars make a good standby when fresh leaves or flowers are not in season.

Sweet cicely

Brandy

Sugar

Butter

Apricots

CLAFOUTIS OF APRICOTS

This rustic dish from central France is most often made with cherries, but it is good with other fruit such as apricots or plums. The flavors of lemon verbena or balm also complement apricots; for plums, try mint. If you have a suitable herb sugar (see page 125), use it in the clafoutis.

INGREDIENTS

1lb (500g) ripe apricots
2 tbsp butter
¼ cup (75g) sugar
3 tbsp brandy or dark rum
2 tbsp finely chopped sweet cicely
1 cup (250ml) light cream or milk
3 eggs
½ cup (60g) all-purpose flour, sifted
confectioners' sugar, to decorate
sprig of lemon verbena or mint, to decorate

PREPARATION

1 Cut the apricots in half and remove the pits. Heat the butter in a large skillet and cook the fruit over low heat with 3 tablespoons of sugar for 10 minutes. The apricots should still hold their shape.
2 Remove from the heat, add the brandy and the sweet cicely, and let soak for 30 minutes.
3 Heat the oven to 400°F/200°C. Transfer the apricots, cut side uppermost, to a shallow 4–5 cup (1–1½ liter) ovenproof dish.
4 Purée the cream, remaining sugar, eggs, flour, and juices from the fruit at high speed in a blender. Pour over the fruit and bake for 30–35 minutes, until the clafoutis is puffed up and lightly browned.
5 Serve warm rather than hot, sprinkled with confectioners' sugar. Decorate with lemon verbena.
KCal 427 P 9g C 44g S 144mg SFA 13g UFA 8g

*Light
cream*

Eggs

Flour

*Confectioners'
sugar*

*Lemon
verbena*

LAVENDER ICE CREAM

An ice cream with a rich, soft texture and a delicate yet distinct taste of lavender. Illustrated on page 126. Serves 4—6.

INGREDIENTS

scant 1 cup (200ml) water
1 cup (200g) sugar
30 lavender flowers
4 egg yolks
1⅓ cups (300ml) heavy cream
2 egg whites

PREPARATION

1 Put the water and sugar in a heavy pan and bring slowly to a boil. Simmer for 5 minutes and remove from the heat. Infuse the lavender in the syrup and let stand until cool, then strain.
2 Whisk the egg yolks until pale and creamy. Pour in the syrup in a steady stream, still whisking.
3 Beat the cream until it holds soft peaks and stir into the mixture. Beat the egg whites until stiff and fold them in. Churn in an ice cream machine for 15 minutes, then put in the freezer. If you do not have a machine, set the freezer to its lowest setting at the start, pour the mixture into an ice cube tray, and freeze. When set around the sides and on the bottom, pour into a chilled bowl and beat vigorously. Return to the tray and freeze. Repeat the process once more so that no large ice crystals form.
KCal 590 P 5g C 55g S 63mg SFA 24g UFA 14g

ROSE GERANIUM ICE CREAM

INGREDIENTS

1¼ cups (300ml) milk
12 rose-scented geranium leaves
3 egg yolks
¼ cup (75g) sugar
1¼ cups (300ml) heavy or whipping cream

PREPARATION

1 Heat the milk almost to boiling, remove, and infuse the geranium leaves for an hour.
2 Beat the egg yolks and sugar until thick and pale.
3 Strain the milk, discarding the leaves. Gently reheat it and beat a little into the yolks. Pour the egg mixture into the milk and return the pan to low heat. Stir until the custard is thick enough to coat the back of a spoon; do not let it boil. Cool.
4 Whip the cream lightly and fold into the custard. Freeze in a freezer or ice cream machine, as above.
KCal 498 P 6g C 25g S 75mg SFA 25g UFA 15g

MINT AND TEQUILA TART

Spearmint is the best kind to use in this tart; the leaves must be young. Serves 4—6.

INGREDIENTS

Shortcrust Pastry
1½ cups (175g) all-purpose flour sifted with pinch of salt
7 tbsp (100g) butter, in pieces
1 egg
1—2 tbsp ice water
Filling
3 eggs
½lb (250g) cream cheese
½ cup (100ml) heavy cream or crème fraîche
¼ cup (60g) sugar
6 tbsp (90ml) tequila
4 tbsp chopped young mint leaves
a few small mint leaves, to decorate

PREPARATION

1 Make the pastry by cutting the butter into the flour to get a crumblike texture. Bind with the egg and water. Let rest for 30 minutes. Roll out and line a 10in (25cm) loose-bottomed tart pan. Set it on a baking sheet. Heat the oven to 350°F/180°C.
2 Combine the ingredients for the filling in a food processor. Taste and add more sugar if you wish.
3 Put the filling in the pastry shell and bake for 20—25 minutes, until the tart is golden and has risen slightly. Serve warm, decorated with mint.
KCal 848 P 14g C 52g S 507mg SFA 37g UFA 20g

RASPBERRY FOOL WITH LEMON BALM

INGREDIENTS

4 sprigs lemon balm
2 tbsp vodka
1 pint (500g) raspberries
⅓ cup (100g) superfine sugar
⅔ cup (150ml) heavy cream
lemon balm leaves, to decorate (optional)

PREPARATION

1 Strip the leaves from the lemon balm and let soak in the vodka for 3—4 hours.
2 Crush the raspberries with a fork, adding the sugar a spoonful at a time. For a smoother texture, purée the raspberries with the sugar.
3 Strain the vodka and stir it into the fruit with the cream. Chill and serve decorated with a few small lemon balm leaves, if you wish.
KCal 317 P 3g C 33g S 11mg SFA 11g UFA 6g

STRAWBERRIES WITH WOODRUFF SABAYON

The sabayon must be whisked until chilled, otherwise it may separate. If you like this dish, try sabayon flavored with a few lavender flowers to accompany blueberries. Illustrated on page 127. Serves 6.

INGREDIENTS

2 sprigs woodruff
⅔ cup (150ml) white wine
3 egg yolks
½ cup (100g) sugar
¼ cup (50ml) orange juice
grated zest of ½ orange
1 pint (500g) strawberries

PREPARATION

1 Infuse the woodruff in the wine for 2–3 hours, then discard the sprigs.
2 Whisk the egg yolks and sugar together in a large bowl until thick and pale. Immerse the bottom of the bowl in a pan of hot, but not boiling, water. Keep whisking and add the wine. After a few minutes' more whisking, the mixture should become frothy and mousselike.
3 Remove from the heat and whisk in the orange juice and zest.
4 Set the bowl over a bowl of ice cubes and continue whisking until the mixture is cold. Serve with the strawberries.
KCal 135 P 2g C 24g S 15mg SFA 1g UFA 1g

ORANGES WITH TARRAGON SYRUP

INGREDIENTS

6 oranges
½ cup (100g) sugar
⅔ cup (150ml) water
6 sprigs tarragon

PREPARATION

1 Peel the oranges, removing all pith. Slice and remove any seeds. Put the oranges in a shallow serving bowl and pour over the juice that has accumulated as they were cut.
2 Heat the sugar and water in a heavy pan. When the sugar has dissolved, simmer for 3 minutes. Infuse 5 tarragon sprigs and leave until lukewarm.
3 Chop the remaining tarragon leaves fine and scatter over the oranges. Strain over the syrup and leave until quite cool, but do not chill.
KCal 188 P 3g C 47g S 12mg SFA 0g UFA 0g

GERANIUM CREAM CHEESE WITH BLACKBERRIES

Illustrated overleaf. If using a coeur à la crème mold, quantities are sufficient to fill two.

INGREDIENTS

½lb (250g) cream cheese
2 egg whites, whipped
3 tbsp geranium-flavored herb syrup (see below)
½ pint (300g) blackberries

PREPARATION

1 Mix the cream cheese with the egg whites and syrup. Line a sieve or mold with damp cheesecloth. Put in the cheese and fold the edges of the cloth over the top. Let drain over a deep bowl for a few hours in the refrigerator or in a cool place.
2 Turn out the cheese onto a serving plate and surround it with the blackberries.
KCal 328 P 4g C 12g S 217mg SFA 19g UFA 10g

HERB SUGAR

Many early cookbooks have instructions for making herb sugars and syrups for flavoring desserts and cakes. Use strong-scented leaves or flowers, such as lavender, lemon balm, lemon verbena, mint, pineapple sage, rosemary, scented geraniums, and violets.

INGREDIENTS

2oz (60g) fresh herb leaves or flowers
¾ cup (200g) sugar

PREPARATION

Put the herb in a cheesecloth bag in the bottom of a jar and add the sugar. Leave in a warm place for 1–2 weeks. Pour off the sugar into another jar and discard the herb bag. The sugar keeps indefinitely.

HERB SYRUP

INGREDIENTS

¾ cup (200g) sugar
⅔ cup (150ml) water
a few fresh herb sprigs, leaves, or flowers

PREPARATION

Bring the sugar and water slowly to a boil. Simmer for 3 minutes. Pour into a jar and immerse the herb. Cover. After a week, discard the herb. Keep the syrup in the refrigerator for up to 3 weeks.
KCal 797 P 1g C 211g S 3mg SFA 0g UFA 0g

*Geranium Cream Cheese
with Blackberries
(see previous page)*

*Lavender Ice Cream
(see page 124)*

*Strawberries with
Woodruff Sabayon
(see page 125)*

DRINKS

Every culture has its herb teas, often taken for their medicinal or digestive properties. Fragrant tisanes have become popular as after-dinner drinks; chilled and poured over ice they are an excellent alternative to the fruit drinks of summer afternoons.

Pineapple Cup

PINEAPPLE CUP

Serves 6–8.

INGREDIENTS

*1 large pineapple, peeled and cored
2¼ cups (600ml) syrup, as for the mango frappé, right
juice of 1–2 limes
4½ cups (1 liter) still or sparkling water
sprigs of pineapple sage*

PREPARATION

1 Purée the pineapple. Bring the syrup to a boil and add it with the motor running, then the lime juice.
2 Let the drink cool, add the water, and serve decorated with sprigs of pineapple sage.
KCal 168 P neg C 44g S 2mg SFA 0g UFA neg

MINT AND LEMON SHERBET

INGREDIENTS

*1¼ cups (300ml) water
½ cup (150g) sugar
large handful of mint leaves, coarsely chopped
4 cardamom seeds, crushed
juice of 1 lemon
still or sparkling water
ice cubes
sprigs of mint, to decorate*

PREPARATION

1 Bring the water and sugar to a boil. Add the mint and cardamom, simmer for 3–4 minutes, then remove the pan from the heat. Cover and let cool. Infuse the mint and cardamom for at least 2 hours.
2 Strain the mixture and add the lemon juice.
3 To serve, dilute the syrup with still or sparkling water to taste, pour it over the ice cubes in individual glasses, and decorate with sprigs of mint.
KCal 155 P 1g C 40g S 3mg SFA 0g UFA 0g

MANGO FRAPPE

INGREDIENTS

*2 cups (500ml) water
¾ cup (200g) sugar
3 ripe mangoes
juice of 1 lemon
sprigs of mint (apple mint is good)*

PREPARATION

1 Make a light syrup by boiling together the water and sugar. Peel the mangoes, then purée the flesh in a blender until coarse. Pour in the boiling syrup with the motor still running, then the lemon juice.
2 Cool and freeze until the frappé is almost solid, but do not let it pass the pouring stage. Crush the mint with a pestle or wooden spoon and add it to the glasses with the frappé.
KCal 273 P 1g C 71g S 3mg SFA 0g UFA 0g

MAY BOWL

This fresh summer drink from Germany is flavored with woodruff, picked before it flowers. Use it sparingly, so the wine does not acquire too strong a flavor. A nonalcoholic May bowl can be made using homemade lemonade or apple juice.

INGREDIENTS

*1 bottle white (preferably German) or sparkling wine
2 sprigs woodruff
2 oranges, peeled and sliced*

PREPARATION

Pour the wine into a bowl or pitcher and add the woodruff and oranges, with any juice from slicing them. Infuse for 10 minutes, then remove the woodruff and serve, over ice cubes if you wish.

MULLED WINE WITH SAGE

This warming wine is based on an old Hungarian recipe.

INGREDIENTS

*½ bottle red wine
2 tbsp torn sage leaves
strip of lemon peel
2–3 tbsp sugar, or to taste
1 cinnamon stick, broken into pieces
juice of 1 lemon, or to taste*

PREPARATION

Heat the wine gently with the sage, lemon peel, sugar, and cinnamon. Bring to a boil, then remove from the heat and stir in the lemon juice.

HERB TEAS

Herb teas or tisanes can be made from a number of wild and garden herbs. Per cup, you usually need 2 tablespoons of a fresh herb or 1 tablespoon of dried, depending on the strength of the herb. Infuse the herb for a few minutes in boiling water, then strain. To make an iced tea, use half the quantity of water, cool, and pour over ice cubes.

Angelica, bergamot, borage, scented geraniums, hyssop, lemon balm, lemon verbena, lovage, mint, marjoram, rosemary, sage and pineapple sage, sweet cicely, thyme, and woodruff all make delightful herb teas.

A good summer tea blend comprises equal parts apple mint, bergamot, and lemon verbena. Fresh lemon balm makes a nice tea and a refreshing cooler when lemon juice is added to taste.

MOROCCAN MINT TEA

The preparation of tea is an art in Morocco: it is made in a tall silver pot and served in small glasses. Makes 3 cups (¾ liter).

INGREDIENTS

*1½ tbsp green tea
handful of Moroccan mint sprigs
½ cup (150g) sugar
approximately 3 cups (750ml) boiling water*

PREPARATION

1 Put the green tea in the pot and pour on a little boiling water. Swirl it around and then pour it out again, keeping the leaves in the pot. This helps remove the dust from the tea and some of the bitterness.

2 Add the sprigs of mint and the sugar to the pot and pour in the boiling water. Let steep for about 5 minutes. Be sure to push down any mint that rises to the surface, or it will give the tea an unpleasant taste.

3 To serve, pour into small glasses and offer more sugar, preferably lump sugar, if necessary.

VARIATIONS

Moroccans also make infusions of herbs such as lavender, lemon verbena, and mint. These are sweetened with sugar and drunk either hot or cold as digestive aids.

*Moroccan
Mint Tea*

BREADS

A number of traditional breads, such as the Tuscan rosemary bread shown below right, are flavored with herbs, but there is plenty of opportunity for the home baker to experiment with different herbs and grains to produce an even wider range. For example, try adding fresh fenugreek to an Indian nan. If you have some herb bread left over, use it for making croutons for salads and soups.

CORN BREAD WITH PARSLEY AND BASIL

Corn bread is quick to make and is best eaten hot as an accompaniment to a main dish.

INGREDIENTS

1 cup (125g) cornmeal
⅓ cup (50g) all-purpose flour
½ cup (50g) oatmeal
3 tsp baking powder
½ tsp salt
2 tbsp poppy seeds
2 tbsp chopped flat-leaf parsley
2 tbsp chopped basil
3 eggs, well beaten
scant 1 cup (200ml) milk
4 tbsp cream
4 tbsp butter, melted

PREPARATION

1 Heat the oven to 400°F/200°C.
2 Mix the cornmeal, flour, oatmeal, baking powder, salt, and poppy seeds in a large bowl. Stir in the herbs.
3 Add the eggs and enough milk to form a thick batter, beating well with a wooden spoon. Stir in the cream and melted butter.
4 Liberally oil an 8–9in (20–23cm) cast-iron skillet, the traditional pan for cooking corn bread, or a similar sized baking dish or cake pan. Pour in the batter and bake for 15–18 minutes. When cooked, a skewer or toothpick inserted in the middle should come out clean.
5 Cut the corn bread into triangles or squares and wrap in a napkin to keep warm. Any leftover pieces can be cut in half and toasted or fried.
KCal 1773 P 58g C 182g S 3017mg SFA 52g UFA 48g
(for total quantity of bread)

Corn Bread

Arab Bread with Zahtar

ARAB BREAD WITH ZAHTAR

This bread is usually baked in flat rounds and the top sprinkled with zahtar, a Middle Eastern herb and spice mixture. Alternatively, it may be coated with a paste of olive oil and zahtar.
(The name zahtar is also given to an herb, similar to thyme, used in Middle Eastern cooking, see page 14.)
In this version I have folded the bread around the flavoring so that less is lost when you cut or break a piece. Sumac is a deep red-purple, coarse powder with a tart flavor, ground from dried sumac berries. It is sold in Middle Eastern stores.

INGREDIENTS

½ envelope instant yeast or 1 tsp ordinary dried yeast
4 cups (500g) bread flour
1 tsp salt
approximately 1¾ cups (400ml) warm water
5 tbsp olive oil
Zahtar
3 tbsp sesame seeds
about 1½ cups (50g) fresh thyme or zahtar leaves (see page 14) or ½ cup (25g) dried
½ cup (25g) sumac

PREPARATION

1 If using instant yeast, sprinkle it over the flour with the salt. Put ordinary dried yeast to prove in a little of the warm water until frothy, then stir it into the flour.
2 Add 4 tablespoons of the oil and enough warm water to mix to a thick batter. Continue to stir for a minute or two, then invert onto a floured work surface and knead until the dough is supple and elastic, about 7–8 minutes.
3 Leave the dough to rise in a lightly oiled bowl covered with plastic wrap. It should double in volume in about 1½ hours.
4 To prepare the zahtar, lightly dry-roast the sesame seeds in a skillet (for method, see page 93) and let cool. Chop the thyme or grind it in a mortar and mix with the sesame seeds, sumac, and remaining olive oil.
5 Punch down the dough, and knead it briefly. Then roll it out on a floured surface into an oblong twice as long as it is wide and about ¼in (5mm) thick. Spread the zahtar lengthwise down the center of the oblong and fold over one side to cover the filling. Press the edge down lightly to seal it. (The shape of the finished bread is something like a German stollen.)
6 Put the bread on a lightly oiled baking pan, cover, and let rise again for 30 minutes.
7 Heat the oven to 400°F/200°C.
8 Bake the loaf for 20 minutes, then reduce the heat to 325°F/160°C and bake for an additional 20–25 minutes. When ready, the bread should sound hollow if tapped on the bottom. Cool on a wire rack.

KCal 2738 P 71g C 385g S 1592mg SFA 16g UFA 89g (for total quantity of bread)

Whole-Wheat Herb Bread (recipe on next page)

Rosemary Bread (recipe on next page)

WHOLE-WHEAT HERB BREAD

The herbs in this bread can be changed to suit your taste, as can the quantities, but choose those that withstand heat well such as sage, oregano, savory, rosemary, lovage, and micromeria. Add seeds if you wish — dill, fennel, and caraway are all excellent in bread. Makes two 1lb (500g) loaves. Illustrated on previous page.

INGREDIENTS

6 cups (750g) whole-wheat flour
2 cups (250g) all-purpose flour
1 envelope instant yeast or 2 tsp ordinary dried yeast
1 tsp salt
approximately 2¼ cups (600ml) warm water
1 tbsp chopped thyme
2 tbsp chopped dill
2 garlic cloves, finely chopped
3 tbsp olive oil, plus some for greasing

PREPARATION

1 Mix the flours together and warm in an oven on the lowest possible setting. Remove and sprinkle on the instant yeast with the salt. If using ordinary dried yeast, put it to prove in a little of the warm water; make a well in the center of the flour and add the mixture after it froths.
2 Add the herbs, garlic, and oil. Mix all well into the flour with enough of the warm water to make a firm yet sticky dough. Knead the dough in the bowl until smooth and elastic, adding a little more flour if necessary. Do not overhandle it.
3 Rinse the bowl, oil it lightly, and return the ball of dough to rise, covered with oiled plastic wrap, until doubled in bulk, about 1½–2 hours.
4 Place the dough on a lightly floured work surface, punch it down, and knead briefly. Cut in half and form into two cylinders. Place on oiled baking sheets or shape them to fit two oiled 1lb (500g) loaf pans, making sure that the seam is underneath. Cover with a cloth or more oiled plastic wrap and let rise for 45–60 minutes, until the dough has almost doubled in bulk.
5 Heat the oven to 400°F/200°C.
6 Bake for 20 minutes, then reduce the heat to 350°F/180°C and bake for 25–30 minutes more, until the bread sounds hollow when tapped on the bottom. If you cannot get the loaves out of the pans, cool them on a rack for 10 minutes. If they then do not sound hollow when tapped, put back on the oven shelf for a few minutes. Let cool.
KCal 3631 P 131g C 671g S 1602mg SFA 9g UFA 48g (for total quantity of bread)

ROSEMARY BREAD

This bread, pan di ramerino, can now be found all year round in Tuscany, but it was originally made for the week before Easter. Italian bakers usually sell rolls rather than whole loaves. These quantities are sufficient for two 1lb (500g) loaves. Illustrated on previous page.

INGREDIENTS

1 envelope instant yeast or 1 tbsp ordinary dried yeast
1kg (2lb) strong white flour
1 tsp salt
leaves from 2 sprigs rosemary, finely chopped
approximately 2¼ cups (600ml) warm water
4 tbsp olive oil, plus some for greasing
½ cup (75g) raisins
1 egg, lightly beaten

PREPARATION

1 If you are using instant yeast, sprinkle it over the flour with the salt and the chopped rosemary, and stir well. If you have ordinary dried yeast, put it to prove in a little of the warm water and add it to the flour, salt, and rosemary when frothy. Make a well in the middle of the flour before adding the liquids – the yeast mixture (if using ordinary dried yeast), the olive oil, and enough of the remaining warm water to mix to a cohesive dough with a wooden spoon.
2 Place the dough on a floured work surface and knead by hand for about 10 minutes, or use the dough attachment of a food processor, until it is very pliable and elastic. Form it into a ball.
3 Rinse out the bowl, oil it lightly, and return the dough. Cover with oiled plastic wrap and let rise until doubled in bulk, about 1–1½ hours.
4 Punch the dough down and knead in the raisins. Cut in half and shape the dough into two rounds. Let rise again on oiled baking sheets (loaves seam side down) for 30 minutes.
5 Heat the oven to 425°F/220°C.
6 Using a razor, slash the top of the loaves in the form of a cross. Brush the tops with egg, then bake the loaves for about 30 minutes, until the bread sounds hollow when tapped on the bottom. Cool on a wire rack.
KCal 4262 P 128g C 807g S 1708mg SFA 12g UFA 59g (for total quantity of bread)

VARIATION

If you wish to make rolls, cut the dough into small pieces and roll into balls. They will need only 15–20 minutes' additional rising time (step 4), and will take 8–10 minutes to bake.

ROTI

This Indian unleavened bread is made with a mixture of chapati or whole-wheat flour and chickpea flour. The cilantro can be replaced by fenugreek, if you prefer.

INGREDIENTS

*1⅔ cups (200g) whole-wheat flour
½ cup (60g) chickpea flour
1 tsp salt
¼ tsp chili powder or ground cayenne
2 tsp garam masala or ground cumin
3 tbsp chopped cilantro leaves
2 tbsp ghee (clarified butter) or oil
scant ½ cup (100ml) yogurt
3–4 tbsp water
ghee, to serve*

PREPARATION

1 Sift the flours together and add the salt, spices, cilantro, ghee, and yogurt. Mix into a firm dough, then add enough water to make it pliable.
2 Knead on a floured work surface for 8–10 minutes until smooth and elastic. Alternatively, make the dough in a food processor: put in the dry ingredients, add the oil and yogurt in a gentle stream while the motor is running, then drizzle in enough water to form the dough into a smooth ball. Process for a few seconds more before removing the dough.
3 Let the dough rest in a lightly oiled bowl, covered with plastic wrap, for about an hour. Knead again briefly, then divide into 10–12 pieces. Shape into balls and keep covered with a cloth.
4 Roll the balls out on a floured surface into circles 5–6in (12–15cm) in diameter and ⅛in (2.5mm) thick. Rotate the disks as you roll them to get an even thickness. Cover with a cloth.
5 Heat a griddle or heavy skillet (with no fat) and cook each roti until the underside is dry and has blisters. Flip it and cook until brown spots show on the surface.
6 To puff up the bread, heat a back burner and put a heat diffuser over it. Put the roti onto the diffuser and it will puff up in a few seconds. Remove to a basket lined with a dish towel and brush lightly with ghee. Fold over the cloth and keep warm.
7 Bake the other breads, removing the griddle or skillet from the heat periodically so that it does not get too hot.
8 Serve warm with Lentils Flavored with Herbs, Indian Style (see page 105), chutneys, and a glass of lassi, the Indian yogurt drink.
KCal 146 P 5g C 17g S 170mg SFA 4g UFA 2g (per roti)

FOCACCIA

Focaccia is an easy bread to make and can be flavored with a number of aromatic herbs. I have used sage here, but thyme, oregano, and rosemary are suitable, too. For the last two reduce the amount to 2 tablespoons. It is best eaten on the day it is made. Makes 1 focaccia.

INGREDIENTS

*½ envelope instant yeast or 1 tsp ordinary dried yeast
3 cups (375g) all-purpose flour
1 cup (250ml) warm water
1 tsp salt, plus coarse salt for finishing
4 tbsp finely chopped fresh sage
2–3 tbsp olive oil*

PREPARATION

1 Sprinkle instant yeast over the flour, or, if using dried yeast, allow it to prove in the warm water.
2 Mix the salt and sage thoroughly with the flour. Add a tablespoon of oil and the water and mix to a soft dough. Remove the dough from the bowl to a floured work surface and knead until it becomes springy and elastic.
3 Rinse the mixing bowl and oil it lightly. Return the dough to the bowl and let it rise, covered with plastic wrap, for about 50 minutes, or until it has doubled in bulk.
4 Heat the oven to 375°F/190°C.
5 Lightly oil a baking sheet. Punch the dough down, knead it a little in the bowl, and then form it into a ball. Put it in the center of the baking sheet and spread it out with your hands to make a circle 1in (2.5cm) thick. Make some indentations in the surface with your fingers and let rise again for 20 minutes, covered with a cloth.
6 Brush the top with olive oil, sprinkle with a little coarse salt, and bake for 40 minutes. Tap the focaccia on the bottom – it will sound hollow when ready. Cool on a wire rack.
KCal 1632 P 48g C 292g S 1571mg SFA 7g UFA 28g (for total quantity of bread)

HERB MIXTURES, MARINADES, RELISHES, AND SAUCES

STORING HERBS

Fresh herbs will keep for a week or more in the refrigerator if packed, not too densely, in an airtight plastic container. They can also be put in plastic bags in the salad drawer, but do not crush the leaves. If you have a bunch of herbs you are going to use in a short time, put them in a pitcher of water in the kitchen and enjoy their fragrance.

Freezing is one of the best methods for preserving herbs. Wash them and dry in a salad spinner and with paper towels, then chop the leaves and store in small plastic containers, or freeze them into ice cubes to store in plastic bags. Most herbs freeze well and retain their fragrance, although they look soft and wilted.

Drying is the traditional method of preserving herbs for winter; it is particularly suitable for those grown in hot climates, with more intense aromas. Pick the herbs early in the day, remove old or discolored leaves, and tie in bunches. Hang in a warm place, out of direct sunlight, until the leaves feel dry and crumble if rubbed. Strip the leaves and store them in jars. A microwave is the most efficient way of drying herbs. Wash and dry the herbs as above and scatter two handfuls of leaves or sprigs evenly on a thick layer of paper towels. Microwave at 100 percent for 4 minutes. (Bay leaves may take slightly longer.) Let cool, then store in jars. For drying, fennel, lovage, mint, rosemary, sage, savory, tarragon, and thyme are best picked before flowering; hyssop, marjoram and oregano should be picked in flower.

Garlic purée Cover 6 whole garlic heads with boiling water. Simmer 15–20 minutes until soft. Drain and let cool, remove the skins, and blend in a food processor or push through a fine sieve. Add a little salt and 4 tablespoons olive oil. Put into a jar and add 4 tablespoons olive oil to seal. Cover with an airtight lid and refrigerate. Use to flavor soups, sauces, and vegetable purées. The garlic goes well with roast lamb, or can be spread on toast and topped with chopped herbs or tomatoes.

FRESH HERB MIXTURE

Stir into vegetable stews, or rub onto lamb or pork.

INGREDIENTS

small sprig rue
2 sprigs mint
2 sprigs oregano
2 sprigs thyme
3–4 lovage leaves
6 sprigs parsley

Purée the herbs in a mortar; the mixture will keep for 2–3 days in the refrigerator.

HERBES DE PROVENCE

Use in daubes (braised meat dishes) and game dishes, and with root vegetables.

INGREDIENTS

4 tbsp dried thyme
2 tbsp dried marjoram
1 tbsp dried rosemary
2 tbsp dried savory
1 tbsp dried lavender flowers
1 tbsp dried hyssop
3 bay leaves

Grind all the herbs together. Remove any large pieces and then store in an airtight jar.

FRENCH MIXTURE

Use with fish, chicken, lentils, and mushrooms.

INGREDIENTS

2 tbsp dried tarragon
2 tbsp dried winter savory
2 tbsp dried marjoram
2 tbsp dried thyme

Grind the ingredients together. Remove any large pieces and store in an airtight jar.

Bouquet for Poultry   *Bouquet for Game*   *Bouquet for Meat*

BOUQUETS GARNIS

A bouquet garni is a little bundle of herbs used to flavor slowly cooked dishes. The herbs are tied with a long string so that they are easily removed at the end of cooking, or they can be enclosed in cheesecloth. A standard bouquet is made up of a few sprigs of thyme, a bay leaf, and 2–3 parsley stalks, but it can be varied to suit the dish and the inclinations of the cook. Here are a few suggestions.

Three variations for fish
Tarragon, thyme, parsley, and lemon peel.
Fennel, bay, and lemon thyme.
Dill, scallions or Welsh onions, parsley, and mint.
Three variations for poultry
Parsley, bay, tarragon, and bruised lemongrass.
Summer savory, marjoram, and rosemary.
Thyme, sage, allspice, and lemon peel.
Five variations for meat
Parsley, thyme, garlic, and bay.
Lovage, parsley, and lemon thyme.
Oregano, orange peel, thyme, and bay.
Rosemary, mint, winter savory, and marjoram.
Celery, Hamburg parsley, thyme, and sage.
Two variations for game
Parsley, juniper berries, thyme, and bay.
Rosemary, orange peel, marjoram, and balm.

HERB GARNISHES

To add a crisp, fresh taste to a dish, a southern European cook will stir in or scatter over a finely chopped aromatic garnish just before serving. This will enliven any simply cooked meat, fish, grain, or vegetable dish, or lift a winter soup or stew. In France it would be a *persillade*, in Italy a *gremolata*. The latter is the classic addition to *osso buco* but the lemon zest gives it a liveliness that suits oily fish as well. Many Catalan recipes are finished with a *picada*, which also thickens the dish.

Persillade Finely chop together a handful of flat-leaf parsley and 2 garlic cloves.
Gremolata Chop and mix together a handful of flat-leaf parsley, 2 garlic cloves, and the grated rind of half a lemon.
Picada Pound or blend together 2 garlic cloves, a handful of flat-leaf parsley, ½ cup (60g) toasted hazelnuts, almonds, or pine nuts, 1 tablespoon toasted bread crumbs (optional), pinch of saffron (optional). Thin the mixture with a little stock from the dish, sherry, or water. Stir in before serving.

FRIED HERB SPRIGS

These make a splendid little treat, and are a classic accompaniment for meat, fish, and omelets. Curly parsley, chervil, sage, chives — especially Chinese chives, cut in short lengths — are good. They must be eaten immediately.

PREPARATION

1 Pick the herbs just before frying, and wash and dry them thoroughly.
2 Heat some oil to about 325°F/160°C in a deep fryer (if it gets too hot the herbs will burn). Put in a few sprigs at a time, in a frying basket or loose.
3 Lift out the herbs as soon as they stop sizzling – they should be ready after about 1 minute – and drain them on paper towels.

HERB VINEGARS

Herb vinegars are useful for dressings, sauces, and marinades. Use fresh herbs, picked early in the day before the sun draws out the aromatic oils, and wine, cider, or rice vinegars. Most flowering herbs are milder than those picked earlier in the season, but flower sprigs can be put into the finished bottles for their decorative effect.

To make herb vinegars, use approximately 2 cups (60g) of the herb to 2 cups (500ml) vinegar. Crush the sprigs or leaves to bring out their flavor, put them in a glass jar, and cover with vinegar. Let steep for three weeks (the flavors develop more quickly if kept in the sun), then strain the vinegar into sterilized bottles. Put a fresh sprig of the herb into each bottle – it strengthens the flavor as well as serving as identification. Use bottles with corks or plastic-lined caps. Vinegars will keep for several years, becoming mellower and sweeter as they age.

Suitable herbs: Basil, borage, burnet, chives, dill, garlic, lavender, lemon balm, lemon verbena, mint, nasturtium flowers, rosemary, tarragon, thyme, and violets. Chilies, lemon zest, peppercorns and seeds of coriander, dill, fennel, and mustard can be used as additional flavorings.

Lemon vinegar: Use a mixture of lemon balm, lemon thyme, lemon verbena, crushed lower part of 2–3 lemongrass stalks, and peel of 2 lemons.

Garrigue vinegar: Use a mixture of winter savory, thyme, rosemary, and bay leaves with 1–2 cloves of garlic and 1–2 dried chilies.

Summer salad vinegar: Use a combination of basil, borage, chives, and tarragon.

HERB OILS

The best herbs to use are basil, bay, dill, fennel, garlic, lemongrass, mint, oregano, rosemary, savory, and thyme. Dried chilies or peppercorns and the seeds of anise, cumin, dill, or fennel may be added.

To make herb oils, use 3–4 tablespoons or 4–6 sprigs of the herb to 2 cups (500ml) oil. Use virgin olive, light sunflower, or grape-seed oil. Put the herbs in a sterilized jar, pour over the oil, close, and let stand for 2–3 weeks. Strain into a sterilized bottle and label. Herb oils will keep for up to a year if stored in a cool, dark place.

HERB BUTTERS

These can accompany grilled fish, poultry or meat, and most vegetables, and are good for making sandwiches. Many herbs make successful butters. Serve basil butter with baked or grilled tomatoes or mushrooms; burnet butter enlivens a dish of lentils; chive butter is a good accompaniment for peas and snow peas. Dill or fennel butter goes well with any fish or with a dish of lima beans, marjoram butter with kidney beans or broccoli, mint and mint-scented marigold with carrots, peas, grilled lamb. Parsley (*maître d'hotel*) butter is traditionally served with grilled steak and on boiled new potatoes; it is also excellent with zucchini. Tarragon butter can accompany pumpkin. A butter made with a mixture of dill and lemon verbena goes well with zucchini, green beans, or fish.

To make herb butters, soften 10 tablespoons (150g) butter with a fork and beat in 1–2 tablespoons lemon juice and 4–6 tablespoons chopped herbs. When well blended, shape the butter into a long roll, wrap in foil, and refrigerate until needed. Herb butters can be frozen for a few months. Try adding paprika, cayenne, ground pepper, garlic, or shallot.

Herb Oil and Garrigue Vinegar

MARINADES

Marinades are an important element in preparing meat or fish to be grilled, roasted, or fried; they tenderize and enhance flavor and also help preserve the food. They are usually liquid, but Latin American and Mexican cooks also use pastes, called *adobos*, which are rubbed onto the food.

To marinate food, mix the marinade ingredients together in a container that will not react with acid (for instance, glass or ceramic). Immerse the meat or fish, turning it from time to time. Put the food in the refrigerator, but bring it to room temperature before cooking. Meat should be marinated for 3–4 hours and can stand overnight; fish and shellfish need only 1–2 hours. Use the marinade to baste the food while cooking. If it is suitable for serving as a sauce, first bring it to a boil and boil hard for a few minutes to kill any bacteria from the raw meat or fish. Never reuse a marinade.

CHIMICHURRI

This marinade and sauce for grilled meat comes from Argentina, where it is most commonly used with steaks. Marinate the meat in some of the chimichurri, reserving the rest to serve as a sauce.

INGREDIENTS

4 garlic cloves, finely chopped
1 tsp black peppercorns, crushed
2 tsp oregano leaves
1 bay leaf, crumbled
6 tbsp chopped flat-leaf parsley
1–2 tsp chili flakes
scant ½ cup (100ml) olive oil
⅓ cup (80ml) red wine herb vinegar

AN ASIAN MARINADE

Use for spare ribs, poultry, or fish.

INGREDIENTS

6 tbsp (90ml) rice wine vinegar
⅔ cup (150ml) fish sauce
juice of 2 limes
4 tbsp sunflower oil
2 shallots, chopped
2 garlic cloves, chopped
small piece of fresh ginger, chopped
2 tsp sugar
1 fresh chili, sliced, or 1 dried chili, crushed
4 tbsp chopped cilantro – root, leaf, and stalk

RED WINE MARINADE

Use for game and large cuts of meat. In Germany, a few sprigs of woodruff might replace the rosemary and thyme.

INGREDIENTS

½ bottle red wine
1 tbsp olive or sunflower oil
1 sprig rosemary
2–3 stalks thyme
2 bay leaves
1 onion, sliced
4 allspice berries, crushed

YOGURT MARINADE

Use for lamb or beef that is to be grilled.

INGREDIENTS

1¼ cups (300ml) plain yogurt
4 tbsp olive or sunflower oil
1 garlic clove, crushed
1 small onion, grated
¼ tsp paprika or cayenne
2 tbsp each basil and mint

SEAFOOD MARINADE

The alcohol enhances the flavor of the fennel.

INGREDIENTS

⅔ cup (150ml) white wine
3 tbsp lemon juice
3 tbsp Pernod, ouzo, or dry anís
3 tbsp olive or sunflower oil
handful of fresh fennel leaves and stalks

A NEW MEXICAN ADOBO

Use for pork, beef, or fillets of firm-fleshed fish. Purée all the ingredients in a food processor.

INGREDIENTS

6–8 dried chilies, toasted (see page 92)
4 garlic cloves, chopped
1 small onion, chopped
a few black peppercorns, crushed
2 bay leaves, crumbled
1 tbsp dried Mexican or European oregano
2 tsp thyme
juice of 1 orange
juice of ½ lemon

SALSAS, RELISHES, CHUTNEYS, AND SAUCES

These provide a good way of adding herb flavors to simply cooked foods, such as poached fish or grilled meat. Several of the salsas and sauces in preceding recipes can be used with other dishes — for instance, herb and horseradish sauces, page 79; salsa cruda, page 84; salsa fresca, page 92; lemon balm salsa, page 93; and béarnaise and paloise sauces, page 101. *Nutritional information for each of the following recipes is for the total quantity.*

PARSLEY, ONION, AND ORANGE SALSA

A refreshing salsa for roast or grilled meats.

INGREDIENTS

2 cups (60g) curly parsley, chopped
1 small red onion, chopped
1 garlic clove, chopped
juice of 2 oranges
juice of 2 lemons
4 tbsp olive oil

PREPARATION

Mix all the ingredients together. The salsa can be kept, covered, in the refrigerator for up to 2 days.
KCal 676 P 4g C 29g S 44mg SFA 8g UFA 49g

RED PEPPER RELISH

This relish from the Balkans usually accompanies meats or fried fish, but it is also good spread on crusty bread.

INGREDIENTS

6 large garlic cloves
2 onions, quartered
6 red peppers, skinned, seeded, and chopped (see page 102)
thinly grated rind of 1 lemon
3½ cups (100g) flat-leaf parsley, chopped
scant 1 cup (200ml) sunflower oil
¼ cup (60ml) red wine vinegar

PREPARATION

Blanch the garlic and onions in boiling water, then drain and chop. Add the red peppers, lemon rind, and parsley. Whisk the oil and vinegar together and pour over the peppers. Mix well, then pour into a clean bowl or jar and chill for several hours. The relish will keep for up to a week in the refrigerator.
KCal 2488 P 24g C 135g S 123mg SFA 26g UFA 170g

LOVAGE AND LIME RELISH

An ideal relish for grilled fish, chicken, or pork.

INGREDIENTS

5 tbsp chopped lovage
1½ tsp ground cumin seeds
1—2 green chilies, seeded and chopped
5 tbsp lime juice
4 tbsp olive oil

PREPARATION

Combine all the ingredients. The relish will keep, if covered, for up to 2 days in the refrigerator.
KCal 562 P 4g C 3g S 34mg SFA 9g UFA 50g

CILANTRO CHUTNEY

A fresh, sharp-tasting chutney to serve as an accompaniment to Indian dishes.

INGREDIENTS

8 cups (250g) cilantro leaves and young stalks
1—2 green chilies, seeded and chopped
2 garlic cloves, chopped
½ cup (60g) sesame seeds, dry-roasted (see page 93)
2 tbsp sugar
2 tsp salt
1 cup (250ml) white wine vinegar, or cider vinegar

PREPARATION

Purée together in a food processor the cilantro, chilies, garlic, and sesame seeds. Scrape down the sides of the container from time to time. Add the sugar, salt, and vinegar, and blend again. The chutney will keep in the refrigerator for a few weeks.
KCal 541 P 18g C 38g S 3241mg SFA 5g UFA 28g

PESTO

This sauce is now a classic. Try different basils — both lemon and African Blue basil are good — or replace the basil with cilantro, mint, or arugula, and the pine nuts with walnuts. Follow the instructions for making pistou on page 50: add the nuts with the basil and garlic.

INGREDIENTS

6 large handfuls of basil leaves
3 tbsp pine nuts
3 garlic cloves, crushed with a little salt
¼ cup (60g) freshly grated Parmesan or romano cheese
approximately ¾ cup (180—200ml) olive oil
KCal 2394 P 45g C 27g S 1086mg SFA 40g UFA 180g

Lovage and Lime Relish

Red Pepper Relish

Frankfurt Green Sauce

FRANKFURT GREEN SAUCE

INGREDIENTS

⅔ cup (150ml) olive oil
2–3 tbsp herb vinegar
1 tbsp Dijon mustard
3½ cups (100g) mixed herbs such as borage, chervil,
chives, dill, parsley, salad burnet, savory, sorrel, and
tarragon, finely chopped
salt and black pepper
1 tsp sugar
3 hard-cooked eggs, chopped

PREPARATION

Whisk together the oil, vinegar, and mustard. Stir
in the herbs. Season and add the sugar and egg. Serve
with cooked meats, baked or poached fish, or salads.
KCal 1645 P 23g C 10g S 692 mg SFA 26g UFA 132g

SALSA VERDE

INGREDIENTS

1 bunch flat-leaf parsley
a few basil, mint, or calamint leaves
1 garlic clove, crushed
4 anchovy fillets, chopped
1 tbsp capers, chopped
scant 1 cup (200ml) olive oil
salt and black pepper

PREPARATION

Purée the herbs, garlic, anchovies, and capers with
a few tablespoons of oil. With the processor motor
running, slowly add the remaining oil and season.
Serve with poached fish and boiled meats. In Italy,
regional variations include other herbs, hard-cooked
egg yolks, or bread crumbs soaked in vinegar.
KCal 1895 P 9g C 4g S 913mg SFA 28g UFA 139g

SAUCE MESSINE

INGREDIENTS

1 lemon
2 tbsp chopped chervil
2 tbsp chopped parsley
2 tbsp chopped tarragon
2 shallots, chopped
1¼ cups (300ml) heavy cream
2 tbsp butter
2 egg yolks

PREPARATION

Grate the rind of half the lemon and mix with the
herbs and shallots. Put the mixture into a heavy pan
or the top of a double boiler with the cream, butter,
and egg yolks. Heat gently, whisking constantly, for
10–15 minutes, until the sauce thickens. Do not
let it boil. Squeeze the lemon and stir in the juice
to taste. This sauce is excellent with poached fish.
KCal 980 P 17g C 22g S 412mg SFA 55g UFA 30g

SALMORIGLIO

INGREDIENTS

⅔ cup (150ml) olive oil
¼ cup (60ml) hot water
juice of 2 lemons
1 tsp dried or 1 tbsp fresh chopped oregano
2 tbsp chopped flat-leaf parsley
black pepper and salt

PREPARATION

Beat the oil in the top of a double boiler, gradually
adding hot water. Whisk in the lemon juice and herbs
and season. Heat gently and beat until smooth. Pour
over grilled fish, roast meat, or green vegetables.
KCal 1381 P 2g C 5g S 12mg SFA 21g UFA 122g

INDEX

USEFUL ADDRESSES

HERB INFORMATION
Herb Society of America
9019 Kirtland Chardon Road
Kirtland, OH 44094
Tel: (216) 256-0514
Publications, events, and advice for members.

HERB NURSERIES
Nichols Herbs and Rare Seeds
1190 N. Pacific Highway
Albany, OR 97321
Tel: (541) 928-9280
Mail-order plants (April-June), seeds, and herbal products.

Well-Sweep Herb Farm
205 Mt. Bethel Road
Port Murray, NJ 07865
Tel: (908) 852-5390
Wide range of herbs, including many unusual types.

Taylor's Herb Garden, Inc.
1535 Lone Oak Road
Vista, CA 92083
Fax: (619) 727-3485
Plants and seeds by mail order.

Plants of the Southwest
1812 Second Street
Santa Fe, NM 87501
Tel: (505) 438-8888
Plants for warmer climates.

Logee's Greenhouses
141 North Street
Danielson, CT 06239
Tel: (860) 774-8038
Hard-to-find herb plants.

Sandy Mush Herb Nursery
316 Surrett Cove Road
Leicester, NC 28748-9622
Tel: (704) 683-2014
Plants, seeds, books, by mail order.

Companion Plants
7247 N. Coolville Ridge Road
Athens, OH 45701
Tel: (614) 592-4643
More than 500 herb plants, seeds, and fresh cut herbs (retail only).

DRIED HERBS AND SPICES
Penzeys
PO Box 1448
Wankesha, WI 53187
Tel: (414) 574-0277
Mail-order specialists for a wide range of dried herbs and spices.

The Spice House
1031 N. Old World Third Street
Milwaukee, WI 53203
Tel: (414) 272-0977
Interesting range of dried herbs and spices.

SEED SUPPLIERS
Johnny's Selected Seeds
310 Foss Hill Road
Albion, ME 04910
Tel: (207) 437-4301
Heirloom and unusual herb seeds and plants.

ASIAN FOODS
Tsang & Ma
PO Box 5644
Redwood City, CA 94063
Large selection of Chinese herb and vegetable seeds.

SOUTHWESTERN FOODS
Horticultural Enterprises
PO Box 810082
Dallas, TX 75381-0082
Chilies, Mexican herbs, and vegetables.

BIBLIOGRAPHY

Bond, R., articles in *Petits Propos Culinaires*, 30 and 34, London, 1988, 1990
Boulestin, X. M., and Hill, J., *Herbs, Salads and Seasonings*, London, 1930
Bremness, L., *The Complete Book of Herbs*, London, 1988
Cost, B., *Asian Ingredients*, London, 1990
David, E., *Spices, Salt and Aromatics in the English Kitchen*, London, 1970
David, E., *Summer Cooking*, London, 1955
Evelyn, J., *Acetaria*, London, 1699
Gerard, J., *The Herball*, London, 1633 edition
Goldstein, D., *The Georgian Feast*, New York, 1993
Gordon, L., *A Country Herbal*, Exeter, 1980

Grieve, M., *Culinary Herbs and Condiments*, New York, 1971
Grieve, M., *A Modern Herbal*, London, 1931
Halici, Nevin Halici's *Turkish Cookbook*, London, 1989
Hutson, L., *The Herb Garden Cookbook*, Houston, 1992
Kalças, E., *Food from the Fields*, Izmir, 1984
Kennedy, D., *The Cuisines of Mexico*, New York, 1972
Kitchiner, W., *The Cook's Oracle*, London, 1817
Landry, R., *Les Soleils de la Cuisine*, Paris, 1967
Leyel, C. F., *Salads*, London, no date
Leyel, C. F., *Summer Drinks and Winter Cordials*, London, 1925
Loewenfeld, C., and Back, P., *The Complete Book of Herbs and Spices*, Newton Abbot, 1974

Olney, R., *Simple French Food*, London, 1981
Ortiz, E., *The Best of Caribbean Cooking*, London, 1975
Parkinson, J., *Paradisi in Sole*, London, 1656 edition
Parkinson, J., *Theatrum Botanicum*, London, 1640
Pruthi, J. S., *Spices and Condiments*, New Delhi, 1976
Raper, E., *The Receipt Book*, London, 1924
Rodale's *Illustrated Encyclopedia of Herbs*, Emmaus, PA, 1987
Roden, C., *A New Book of Middle Eastern Food*, London, 1985
Rohde, E. S., *Culinary and Salad Herbs*, London, 1940
Rohde, E. S., *A Garden of Herbs*, London, 1926
Rohde, E. S., *Herbs and Herb Gardening*, London, 1936

Rundell, E., *A New System of Domestic Cookery*, London, 1843 edition
Shaida, M., *The Legendary Cuisine of Persia*, Henley, 1992
Smires, L. B., *La Cuisine Marocaine*, Paris, 1971
Sotti, M. L., and Beffa, M. T., *Le Piante Aromatiche*, Milan, 1989
Stobart, T., *Herbs, Spices and Flavourings*, London, 1970
Teubner, C., *Kräuter und Knoblauch*, Fussen, 1993
Tsuji, S., *Japanese Cooking*, Tokyo, 1980
Uyldert, M., *De Taal der Kruiden*, Naarden, 1971
Verral, W., *A Complete System of Cookery*, London, 1759
Vilmorin-Andrieux, *Les Plantes Potagères*, Paris, 1925
White, F., *Flowers as Food*, London, 1934

ACKNOWLEDGMENTS

Author's Acknowledgments
Ted Riddell at Cheshire Herbs, Cy Hyde at Well-Sweep Herb Farm, Anthony Lyman-Dixon at Arne Herbs provided plants and helpful information on many herbs. The staff at Il giardino officinale di Casola Valsenio gave their time to show me the garden and explain their research. Bart Spices and Darégal Herbs provided herbs in oil and frozen herbs respectively.
The Lancellotti family, particularly Angelo, has been very generous with advice, ideas, and recipes. Gene Bourg gave advice on Acadian and Creole cooking, Richard Hosking sent information on herbs in Japan. Paul Breman checked the text and proofs, Sasha and Elinor Breman tested recipes.
Fay Franklin and Pamela Brown at Dorling Kindersley have been patient, painstaking, and helpful in their editing and Julia Worth has been imaginative and accommodating in her design for the book.

Dorling Kindersley would like to thank Ian O'Leary for his photographs; Emma Brogi for photographic assistance; Sarah Ponder for the artworks; home economists Nicola Fowler, Sunil Vijayakar, and Oona van den Berg; Laura Jackson, Clare Marshall, Anna Hagenbuch, and Jennie Dooge for design assistance; Jasmine Challis for nutritional information; Sarah Ereira for the index; Suzy Dittmar, Bridget Roseberry, and Paul Wood for DTP work. With thanks to the following companies and individuals for their assistance: Arne Herbs, Chelsea Physic Garden, Cheshire Herbs, Iden Croft Herbs, Poyntzfield Herb Nursery, Suffolk Herbs, The Savill Garden, Culpeper Ltd., Fox's Spices, and Geneviève Lethu, London (for tableware, pages 63–64).

Picture credits All photography by Ian O'Leary except for: Martin Norris, page 40, top.